And Hearts Are Brave Again

And Hearts are Brave Again

BY

WINSHIP STOREY

And when the strife is fierce, the warfare long,
Steals on the ear the distant triumph song,
And hearts are brave again, and arms are strong.
Alleluia!

LONDON : THE EPWORTH PRESS

Published by

THE EPWORTH PRESS

(FRANK H. CUMBERS)

25–35 City Road, London, E.C.1

New York   .   Toronto
Melbourne   .   Cape Town

Set in Monotype Perpetua 12 point
Printed and bound by William Clowes and Sons Ltd
Beccles, Suffolk

To Mother and to May,
both of whom have, throughout the years,
lavished such a wealth of affection upon me
that, should I ever fail in
thoughtfulness, kindliness or courtesy,
I should stand revealed as
one who knew not how to abound

ACKNOWLEDGEMENTS

SOME of the material which has gone to the making of this little book has already appeared in much shorter form in the columns of *The Methodist Recorder*. Although entirely re-written, I should not care for it to go out without making grateful acknowledgement to the Editor of that periodical for his courtesy in so readily granting me permission to include it.

I should also like to thank my Secretary, Miss E. Ellison, for her unfailing helpfulness in the preparation of the typescript.

WINSHIP STOREY

CONTENTS

Part One

CHAPTER I

INTERPRETATION OF A HANDICAP

THIS is a book for discouraged people; a book about Dismay and Reassurance and Equipment. Most of our dismay arises from a sense of handicap; most of our re-assurances come from realizing that our handicap is capable of an interpretation which changes its entire nature and changes therefore our entire reaction to it; and, extra-ordinary though it may seem, most of our equipment springs from our handicaps thus understood.

It has been required of us that we live out our lives in a world pitiably shattered and broken, in an age almost spiritually bankrupt, and among a people very largely blind to their real resources. We may be presumed, there-fore, if we do any thinking at all, to know something about the first of our subjects—Dismay. Our sense of handicap is so bewildering that we are conscious of little else. There is so much to put right we scarcely know how or where to start. We are so dismayed, most of us, that we are even suspicious of any voice of reassurance: discount it as wish-ful thinking; brand the encouragers as mere dreamers who are not themselves dismayed because they have never realized what a mess everything is in. We give but little thought to spiritual equipment because the notion never occurs to us that there may be a task allotted to us in clear-ing it up. Somebody ought to do something about it, doubt-less, but we are handicapped folk from whom nothing could possibly be expected. That we are not really sincere in this is evidenced by the keen resentment we would display if anybody else said the same thing about us. We can say it of ourselves because it passes muster for modesty and a commendable absence of egotism. Really it has more of cowardice than modesty about it.

If it be true, however, that we can so come to regard our handicap that it can really cease to be one, it is quite evident that an interpretation of it capable of producing such a transformation is of the greatest value in such days as these. Anyhow, it is worth exploring. If we lay hold of something in our quest the whole of life may be changed for us; and even if we miss the thing after all and this little book proves a failure, we shall be none the worse for having sought. No man was ever the worse for seeking to be better.

A little lad lay on his back on the moor, hands clasped behind his head, his eyes fixed intently upon a far distant speck in the sky. Wound tightly round his fingers and stretching away and away into the blue was a thin yellow string down which came constantly the most exhilarating pull from the kite. It had taken some getting aloft. First it had to be thrown up while his Dad, holding the string, had raced about the moor trying to work it up into the wind. This method had soon fallen into disrepute and had been abandoned in favour of Dad throwing up the kite and the laddie doing the racing about. This was quickly agreed to be a much superior technique, Father being, indeed, quite emphatic on the point.

Once flighted the kite rose steadily. Followed the work of paying out the string and watching him grow smaller and smaller as he got higher and higher. Then, with the string full out save for the hold around wrist and fingers, to lie down on the sward and enjoy him was to enter into a lad's heaven wherein the distant speck in the sky was as the symbol of one's dreams and every tug on the cord a message acutely personal to oneself and shared by none other.

Thus enraptured I began to wrestle with a problem. Here was I—earthbound; there was my kite exploring the heavens. All that kept him down was the kite-string I so securely held. The pull began to assume a new significance; the messages coming so thrillingly down the cord began to speak of efforts to be free from that which bound him and to soar to unknown heights. True, I had been the means of his original ascent—apart from my own efforts he could never have risen a yard; but now I had become his handicap who had once been his helper. To what unimagined stratosphere would he reach if I but gave him his liberty! I began to feel quite sorry for him: began, indeed to invest him with a personality and to regard him as suffering a thwarted and frustrated existence, held back by my brutal and selfish disregard of his ambitions. Soon I began to see myself as a tyrant shamefully denying a struggling slave his opportunity to win through to a larger life. The speck in the heavens had ceased to be a kite; it had become a live thing striving to be free.

I secured the string to my arm while I took out my penknife. I was fond of my kite but it was worth losing him to set him free and watch him vanish into the blue as soon as his handicap was removed. I felt the pull, pull as though it were a prayer for release. With a fervent good-bye I cut the kitestring and lay gazing intently to see the last of him.

My consternation at what happened is indescribable. Loosed from my hold the string whipped away into the air; but almost at once something appeared to go wrong with the kite. He lurched to one side as though some support on which he had relied had suddenly failed him. He lost height; he struggled to recover himself and staggered as one stricken with a mortal wound; he plunged again like some mad thing in torment. He whose position of lofty eminence had been held so steadily, so surely, with no trace of uncertainty in his bearing, was no longer sure of anything, had lost all semblance of control, rocked this way and that like a desperate drowning man with naught to cling to—and all the time falling, falling, with never a hint of regaining what was lost.

I was on my feet now, running like mad to catch him as down he came with sickening ungainly side-slips, who once so proudly rode the shouting wind. He fell in utter helplessness. I had removed his handicap—I picked him up, a ruin.

It was long before I understood what had happened. The great paradox defeated me. Vaguely I grasped the astonishing truth that what had kept him down had really kept him up. The kite-string that had been his handicap had in some strange way been his support. Obviously freedom from all restraint was not the way to keep a kite aloft. There came a day when I discovered that that was true of your soul also—but that was years after. My schoolboy problem was to argue out the mystery, 'Why had the kite been unable to keep up when I had removed the one thing that was keeping him down?' This needed concentration. More in this than meets the eye, obviously. Clearly the first thing to do was to find out what the kite-string actually *did*, anyway. And the pull which I had felt so thrilling, as though I had held the reins of some Pegasus in my hand, which had changed in significance to become the striving of an imprisoned thing for liberty, began to take on yet another interpretation. Why was it that immediately the kite-string was severed the kite became the mere sport of the wind? Could it be that some connection existed between the kite-string and the *attitude* of the kite to the wind? I began to see daylight. So long as the kite was braced against the wind it could climb; so long as it faced squarely that which opposed it, the heights it had reached could be maintained; but once it ceased to resist it ceased to ascend. And, stranger still, the very thing which enabled it to face the opposition, and therefore to climb, and therefore to attain a level of existence quite unthinkable otherwise—was its handicap. Curious parallel with larger issues! It was at this point I began to see the hand of God in the business—but, again, that was years afterwards.

To endeavour to help someone into whose hands this little book may fall similarly to trace the hand of God in a handicapped life is the sole purpose of writing it. We shall look therefore at some dismayed people—great souls all of them, for there is much to be learned from the dismay of great souls. We shall try to trace out the divine plan for bringing into life that bracing element which enables us to climb not only in spite of opposition but by means of it, and which brings reassurance out of dismay. We shall take notice of how even God can be frustrated and His divine plan thwarted, for we must at any rate try to be honest and face up to that pathetic possibility.

And finally, having seen our problem—and been dismayed by it, no doubt—and listened to our Lord and been reassured again, we shall look to our equipment: a sort of spiritual kit-inspection.

Then you will close the book, having come to the end of it, and what you do afterwards will indicate whether you have found it worth reading.

Part Two

Dismay

CHAPTER II

A MAN AGHAST

'Who am I, that I should go?'

MANY years ago a young shepherd was watching his flocks in the barren foothills east of the Gulf of Suez. Like most men of his craft he was a thoughtful, contemplative man, though he had another side to his nature—temper enough on occasion and hot resentment of injustice and the wrongs of others. He later became one of the greatest statesmen of all time, though if you had forecast his future to him as he sat there tending his sheep that day, he would probably have smiled ironically upon the value of your judgement. Yet it was said of him, 'So great a statesman did he become that when he died the State went on without him'. No mean testimony to enduring constructive work.

At the time we catch sight of him, however, he is a person of no great importance. Even the sheep he watches are not his own. And, as a matter of fact, for once in a while he is not even watching them. A strange sight has attracted his attention. A bush has caught fire and is blazing furiously. But, curiously, it is not consumed. As he watches, greatly interested and not a little puzzled, he becomes conscious of the presence of God in that strange way we sometimes do when we come up against something we do not understand. Awed, he takes off his shoes, feeling the place where he stands to be holy ground. He hears the voice of God reminding him of the pitiful plight of his fellow countrymen, slaves in a foreign land. He knows the bitterness

14

of hearing tragic tidings without being able to do any-thing about it—surely the most exquisite torment to any sensitive soul. And then—amazing thing—he, an unknown shepherd, realizes that God is telling him that his inability to do anything about it just isn't true: that he is to go and seek audience with the king who has deported and enslaved his people, demand their release and lead them back to freedom.

The thing is incredible, fantastic, sheer stark madness. An Eastern despot, with power enough to have him executed by raising a finger, to be challenged by a mere peasant! Small wonder the man is dismayed at the prospect of what God requires of him. Who amongst us would be other than daunted by it?

'Who am I,' he cries, aghast, 'that I should go unto Pharaoh and that I should bring forth the Children of Israel out of Egypt?' His sheer inadequacy overwhelms him; the enormity of the task overwhelms him; the breath-taking audacity of the whole mad business overwhelms him. Yet, had he but realized it, his very dismay was his greatest asset at the moment.

The plain if somewhat surprising truth is that a sense of dismay is not a bad thing to start off with. It does set you casting about for resources. It enables you, once your panic has subsided and you sit down soberly to weigh up the position, to credit the Almighty with at least ordinary intelligence. For no intelligent Being would ever call a man to a task in which he is *bound to fail*. So that once you are sure it is God's call, no matter how desperate a venture it appears, you may know that success is at least possible to you. In fact, I doubt whether you can ever know what God can do for desperate men until you are a desperate man. But to be driven hard up against a situation completely beyond you is to force your mind to accept the fact—if you believe in God at all, that is—that the very magnitude of your problem is the measure of your resources. When you are driven forward *by* God, you are driven back *on* God, since none other is sufficient for these things. And if you wonder, whimsically, how a man can be driven forward and driven back at the same time, just reflect for a moment that you are driven back on a God who is Himself moving forward and you will see how it works out.

That is why a sense of dismay is not a bad thing to start off with. The dismay of a great soul is a noble thing. It is far removed from mere problem-consciousness: it only begins with that. It proceeds immediately to God-consciousness, and by that time dismay itself has vanished.

Watch this happen to our young desert shepherd. 'Who am I, that I should go?'

Here is the way God deals with loyal but daunted souls: 'Certainly I will be with thee: and this shall be the token unto thee that I have sent thee: when thou hast brought forth the people out of Egypt ye shall serve God upon this mountain.'

He finds himself called to lead a great liberating movement—but it is to be linked to religion: its dynamic is to be religion, its driving force is to be religion, its impetus will be sustained by religion.

What a word to us in these later days, still battling against forces that would enslave and fetter the human spirit—and, perhaps, not a little dismayed at the prospect which faces us! The great liberating movement of our own day can have no other dynamic than religion, no other driving force, no other sustaining impetus.

'The Truth shall make you free,' said Jesus, Himself the Truth. Might of arms cannot do it—it can chain up a demon, but it cannot make a lover, and so long as the demon remains a demon you are not free any more than he is: you are not free from fear of what may happen if the chain breaks. Diplomacy cannot do it, for freedom cannot rest upon so uncertain a foundation as the art of saying one thing and meaning another, which is what diplomacy has so often meant in the past: you must always be wondering what will happen when the other fellow finds out what you really did mean. Treaties cannot do it, for a treaty is only worth what the integrity of its signatories is worth, and that is a minus quality with some folk who have signed quite a number in our time.

At the final analysis, if politics are not religious they are mere unreliable opportunism; if trade agreements are not religious they are mere advantage-seeking; if international relations are not religious they degenerate into unvarnished exploitation. We will never get out of the ungodly mess we are in until we see that all true statesmanship must have a basis of religion.

The real test faces us as a legacy from the war. For in a world bitter in soul, inflamed in passions, largely destitute in spiritual power as well as in reconstructive material resources, exhausted in energy, ruined, devastated, bewildered—in such a world as this we have to re-establish the things that are true, honourable, just, pure, lovely, and of good report.

It has fallen to us to live our lives in days of the ebb-tide of spiritual energy—and in days so tragic that we have greater need of it than has existed for centuries. Moreover, the last generation lost the flower of its manhood in the First World War and the men who should now be the spiritual leaders of the nation are, for the most part, dead. So the task of the great man falls on the shoulders of the ordinary man, and God knows how many of us feel we are faced with an opportunity far too big for us. We too feel overwhelmed by our own inadequacy and the immensity of our task. We cannot but realize, if we will but face the tragic possibility, that it is possible to leave even a defeated enemy still with a belief in force, having learnt nothing from the recent colossal struggle except that, strong as he was, he was not strong enough: and to leave a victorious ally with a still more plausible argument.

That is a prospect dreadful enough to dismay anybody. Of the highest importance is it, therefore, that we do not miss the value, the benefit of our dismay. For only as *your* problem-consciousness gives place to an overpowering sense of God being with you will you pull your weight in the grim business your generation has to put through.

CHAPTER III

A MAN ALONE

'I, even I only, am left'

HERE is another great soul in the grip of dismay. A different type of man this: not much of the thoughtful, contemplative, constructive statesman about him. Inflammable stuff here. A man of fierce, implacable denunciations —plenty of bite about this Tishbite. A man undaunted by odds of four hundred and fifty to one in the dramatic doings on Mount Carmel, but who scoffs and mocks and gibes at his adversaries in the most outrageous way. 'The God that answereth by fire, let him be God!' It is the suggestion of a man whose very religion is fierce flame. A terrible man in the day of God's power, relentless in his hatred of those who defied God. Not the kind of man you would expect to find dismayed.

But the excitement of Carmel dies away. The thrilling occasion passes, with all its evidence of God's response to audacious faith. The crowds go and the aftermath of anticlimax descends. With it comes spiritual and nervous reaction—the right moment for the damaging counterattack of evil. Jezebel chooses her time shrewdly. The man who rose to such heights of fearless leadership in the exhilarating atmosphere of immense crowds is now alone. The opposition is no longer a company of fanatics yelling and leaping and cutting themselves with knives—an exciting spectacle, especially as they become increasingly desperate when hour after hour nothing happens in response— but is now the cold, vindictive, merciless, and utterly unscrupulous hatred of a very clever woman—and a queen at that.

Suddenly he feels terribly alone—abandoned. Amazingly he loses his nerve. Panic seizes him. He is not even a shadow of his former self. It is hard to recognize him as the same man, so absolutely broken and dismayed is he. 'I, even I only, am left and they seek my life to take it away.'

The queen is an expert in conducting a 'war of nerves'. Such warfare has a sadistic technique all its own. 'One by one' is its policy towards its victims. To separate men so that unity is destroyed—strength is destroyed—fellowship is destroyed, and they each suddenly realize that alone and unsupported they must face their mighty enemy—this is to bring upon them a sense of dismay positively paralysing in its effect. Spiritual panic gets hold of them. Few things so sap the confidence of men as to realize or to believe there remains no one of kindred spirit, none of like vision, none of similar fine purpose. That is dismay at its worst. Such bewildered souls cannot even do what they might do. Nothing remains but to throw up the sponge. 'I, even I only, am left and they seek my life to take it away.'

As with men, so with nations. We remember that 'one by one' was the devilish Nazi method. No time for the victims to unite in co-ordinate effort. Any suggestion of doing so on the part of any one small nation brought a snarl and, in a day or two, the big battalions on the frontier. Sweeping over them came the chill flood of dismay—this appalling sense of abandonment and utter helplessness: the utter futility of attempting anything.

War of nerves indeed! We are proud to belong to the one nation that faced it out alone—though in justice to some others we do not lose sight of twenty-one miles of sea which we had on our frontier and they had not on theirs. They had not the good fortune to live on a . . .

> *. . . precious stone set in the silver sea,*
> *Which serves it in the office of a wall*
> *Or as a moat defensive to a house,*
> *Against the envy of less happier lands.*

But there it is—'one by one': the same technique with
nations as with men; separating them, destroying their
unity, breaking their fellowship, bringing them to believe
there remains none of kindred spirit, none of like vision,
none of similar purpose. And alone—or believing themselves to be—they just break. 'I, even I only, am left and
they seek my life to take it away.'

History has seen nothing like the flood-tide of devilry
that inundated Europe in 1940. And we all know that is how
it was done.

So, too, with the Church. Probably none of us has ever
known what it was to belong to a Church which was not
shrinking. Who amongst us can remember the day when the
Christian Church in this country showed any advance in
membership?

'The Church is largely dependent,' says A. J. Gossip,
'on what tired folk give Him in the evening after a full day,'
and it is these loyal, tired folk who get, at long last, de-
spondent and hopeless and dismayed. The folk who do
nothing in the Church feel no dismay: they are always ready
with their trumpery explanations. The preachers cannot
preach, have no message for the times. The people are
snobbish and unfriendly. The Church ought to take more
interest in social questions—or else takes too much interest
in them instead of concentrating on its task of saving souls.
And so on, *ad lib.*—you know it all. No sense of dismay.
The Church has cost them nothing and it could go down
altogether without troubling them much.

No; it is the people who have worked hard and long and
faithfully who get dismayed. Their problems increase as

their numbers diminish. It is like trying to keep back the tide with a broom. Anxiety comes into their service and joy goes out of it. They are left to face difficulties which are not of their making: difficulties largely caused by the defection of others. So they labour on with a growing sense of resentment which eats like a canker into the delight of discipleship that once they knew. How perfectly does Elijah speak for all such in his bitter reply to God in the cave on Horeb.

'What doest thou here, Elijah?'

'What do I here! As if I were a rat deserting a sinking ship! But I am no renegade—not I! I have been very jealous for the Lord the God of Hosts; for the children of Israel have forsaken thy covenant, thrown down thine altars, and slain thy prophets with the sword: and I, even I only, am left; and they seek my life to take it away.'

Only a great soul dare talk thus to God. No traitor this. This is not the kind of man to whom the Church means little—it is his very life. His anger is born of passionate love for the worship of God; his resentment springs from the heartbreak of seeing the dearest thing in the world disintegrate before his very eyes; his dismay is the measure of his loyalty.

Now see the delicate touch of God. He has no rebuke for this exasperated prophet. This man needs no lash—he needs calming, reassuring, hushing; and, above all, he needs fellowship. So in the earthquake God is not to be found— Elijah has had enough of earth-shaking events for the time being. Nor in the fire—God had answered by fire on Carmel's height, but this is a very different occasion. This is the moment for the still, small voice, and beneath its spell all the man's hot resentment fades away. But more than that. Here again is problem-consciousness giving place to God-consciousness—but this man is reassured not only about divine fellowship; he is reassured about human fellowship:

'Do you feel abandoned and discouraged? Problem-conscious to the point of defeat? You are not alone—man alive, you are one of a great host! I have yet seven thousand in Israel which have not bowed the knee to Baal.'

Listen to this still, small voice, you tired, discouraged workers who love the Church, but stand dismayed at the enormous tasks which face her! Listen, you overburdened little company, struggling against mounting indifference and shrinking fidelity! Listen, you heartbroken faithful few, to this still small voice of God! Let not the picture of a shrinking Church depress you to the point of dismay. At the very time when we are witnessing the ebb-tide of Christianity in Europe, the Church in China and India and Africa is embarrassed by its own success. Even if Christianity died out completely in the West, the Faith would not be lost. The growing Churches in the East would keep it going.

The enemies of Christianity must always reckon with the undefeated unknown. God has always His seven thousand. They have not accepted the new order built on savagery and slavery and injustice and barbarism—have not and never will. The Church has always prospered when it has been persecuted. The evil day always calls forth gallant souls ready for high adventure. There is a curious sort of reflex action takes place in times of spiritual crisis. To become more sure of God is to become more aware of kindred souls —and to become more sure of your fellows is to become more aware of God.

That is the second benefit of dismay.

CHAPTER IV

A MAN ASHAMED

'Woe is me! for I am undone; because I am a man of unclean lips, and I dwell in the midst of a people of unclean lips.'

MOSES was a great statesman; Elijah a great prophet. We have seen both dismayed and both delivered from dismay—the one by a fresh experience of divine fellowship; the other by a new awareness of human fellowship. Isaiah combines both types of men—he is the great prophet-statesman. He too came to his desperate hour when he stood dismayed; he too found deliverance from its crippling hold. But in his case, just as he combines both types in his personality and combines both problems in his difficulty, so he finds both solutions combined in his answer. It is divine fellowship within human fellowship that he discovers to be the essential thing—namely, God in the life of the nation.

This is how it came about.

The reign of the greatest king since Solomon had just come to an end, a tragic end. For over fifty years Uzziah had reigned in Jerusalem. It had been an era of great national expansion—something like our own Victorian era; marked by success in war, elaboration of national defence, development of the country's resources. The king's very name means 'Jehovah, his Strength' or 'Jehovah, his Helper', and greatly indeed had he been helped by God. 'Marvellously helped till he was strong,' as the old chronicle has it.

Small wonder if to young Isaiah this great, good king was a fit subject for hero-worship. So wonderful a figure at the head of the nation—such extraordinary prosperity resulting from his leadership—such widespread fame centering round him—such constructive achievements standing to his credit—how could young loyalties be other than aflame in consequence? And in a moment all is swept away.

It is a curious story, and we need to remember that it happened seven centuries before Christ if we would understand it. The king attempts to usurp the functions of the priests and to burn incense in the Temple. No very heinous crime, you say, with your unconscious Protestant background and your belief in the right of every worshipper to approach God direct. We stand upon the word of Jesus to all who labour and are heavy laden to come without the necessity of any intermediary. But not for seven hundred and fifty years did that great message first thrill the hearts of men. Very different were the days of Uzziah. At that time and at that stage in man's spiritual development it was best that men should never forget the remoteness of God. They needed to preserve a sense of awe in the presence of God and the ancient priesthood was God's way of achieving this. Not until man was capable of grasping larger truth did Jesus reveal God as a Father, and then His nearness to us rather than His distance from us was what mattered.

Uzziah was not therefore merely ahead of his time—he was ahead of God's time. Self-display and self-aggrandizement were the motive of his incense-burning. It was an act of presumption. Even so we, with our so very different Christian tradition, find it hard to think ourselves back into the standards of his day and to vindicate the dreadful thing that happened. An unseemly contention breaks out in the Temple between the king and the altar priests. Angry shouts ring through the sacred place—suddenly to be hushed into horrified silence, for on the forehead of the king there flares up the fatal white spot dreaded of all men. Silenced himself by the abrupt hush, realizing that its cause, whatever it was, lay in himself, the king becomes aware of the ghastly truth. He hurries from the Temple a leper and an outcast from his fellows.

Pitiful end to a great reign—fifty years of magnificent leadership, and then this!

To young Isaiah the shock was positively shattering. The news was incredible—impossible—unbelievable: the king in a lazar house; his hero swept in a moment from the throne of immense influence to outcast isolation from his fellow men. All his glory could avail him nothing—disease makes short work of glory. Incredible it might be—but it was true; impossible—it was a fact.

Brooding, perhaps, in the very temple where the horrible business had taken place, struggling to think his way through the collapse of his ideal, two violently conflicting ideas persist in linking up in his mind—wickedness and worship. They have nothing in common, but they unite; they are poles apart, but they come together. His mind revolts at their disgusting association. Intolerable co-operation—he cannot away with it.

But if he be so nauseated—what of God? How must *He* feel about such unholy partnership? In the quiet of the temple it is as though the very voice of God sounds in his ears: 'To what purpose is the multitude of your sacrifices unto me? I am full of the burnt offerings of rams, and the fat of fed beasts; and I delight not in the blood of bullocks, or of lambs, or of he-goats. When ye come to appear before me, who hath required this at your hand, to trample my courts? Bring no more vain oblations; incense is an abomination unto me; new moon and Sabbath, the calling of assemblies —I cannot away with iniquity and the solemn meeting.'

Dismay grips Isaiah's very heart. No great soul can con-template the sin of another without turning the searchlight upon himself. Like eleven loyal fellows in an upper room seven and a half centuries later, he finds rising spontaneously to his lips the cry 'Is it I, Lord?' And like most honest seekers after God, he finds that

> *They who fain would serve Thee best*
> *Are conscious most of wrong within.*

'Woe is me! for I am undone; because I am a man of unclean lips.' Wickedness and worship—it strikes him alike in the temple of his being and in the temple of his God.

But if it be true of the king and if it be true of himself— is it true of the nation at large? This man is a great lover of his nation. He is not seeking companions in condemnation that his own sense of unworthiness may be lessened by others sharing it. Nothing like that. Rather is he bringing his nation before God in confession and remorse. For he finds they are all in it. 'I am a man of unclean lips, and I dwell in the midst of a people of unclean lips.'

Truly the dismay of a great soul this. Just as the great king, 'Jehovah, his Helper', fell from that lofty *dependence* to an ignoble, proud, presuming *independence*, and, astonishingly, even in the very act of worship became alienated from God by the sense of his own importance, so Isaiah feels the national life becoming alienated from God. Jehovah was no longer the national strength: they had become successful and self-sufficient. And even in his own personal life he sees the roots of the same thing.

'True life,' says Forbes Robinson, 'is dependence on God. Sin is isolation, death—a failure to recognize and act on our dependence.' That, in a sentence, is the biography of the great King Uzziah. That, Isaiah was dismayed to find, was the characteristic of his people. Would to God we had left that sort of thing twenty-seven centuries back in history! In his day religion had become a mere parade. In our day it has largely ceased to be anything at all. In his day wicked-ness and worship—in ours, wickedness and no worship. That is not quite true, but much too near the truth to be comfortable. How many of us know a church which is a quarter full? One reads of a company of seven hundred children only two of whom knew what happened on Good Friday. One hears of a man who thought Noah's Ark was Christ's uncle—and did not appear to be trying to be funny. The story of the Prodigal Son is voted 'a jolly good yarn' by people who have never heard it before. One comes across well educated youngsters who have never seen a Bible. This in our own Christian country.

Does not every thinking Christian feel the dismay of this old-world lover of his nation? 'Woe is me! for I am undone; because I am a man of unclean lips, and I dwell in the midst of a people of unclean lips.'

Let us understand his phrase. He does not mean that obscene language was the characteristic either of himself or of his people. But the lips are the medium of expression of a people, and if all they express is the language of pleasure or self-interest, of the market-place or of the sports ground —if the recognition of God and the praises of God are never upon them, then is that man or that people undone, for they are failing to recognize and act on their dependence: they no longer see in God their helper and their strength.

No true lover of our nation can regard unmoved its present paganism. Nor, for that matter, fail to trace some connection between that and the mess we have got ourselves into. I am certainly not one who saw in the war a punish-ment for our national sins. I cannot understand the mentality of those who confuse a struggle for righteousness and the decencies of life with a visitation of divine wrath. But it may well be true that the widespread indifference to religion which is an outstanding characteristic of our age has re-sulted in a general loosening of the moral code throughout all Europe. And is it not almost patent that the general lowering of moral standards has made possible a manner of life which has allowed the seeds of war to take root where otherwise they might have died? After all, worship is but the recognition of 'worth-ship', and if men cease to think the recognition of God worth while they are hardly likely to think much of His laws. So wickedness and worship or wickedness and no-worship (paradoxically enough, the same thing) continue their disintegrating work. And dismay settles on good men.

But as so often happens in the world of the spirit, the sun rises at midnight. 'In the year that King Uzziah died, I saw the Lord,' says Isaiah. In the day when his hero-worship crashed, his faith was born. In the very hour when he realizes most acutely his nation's fatal weakness he is shown the way back to its strength. The human fellowship must be filled with the divine fellowship: the national life must be given a God-contact.

No easy business this, however. In his vision there flew to him one of the seraphim having a live coal in his hand, which he had taken with the tongs from off the altar. 'And he touched my mouth with it, and said, Lo, this hath touched thy lips; and thine iniquity is taken away, and thy sin purged.'

Merely to let your imagination grip the idea is enough to make one cringe. How sensitive to heat are the lips—even a scalding drink can cause exquisite pain. But here is a live coal placed upon them and held there—burning, searing, destroying that which is impure in the very medium of expression, these same lips so sensitive to hurt.

This is the picture Isaiah sees of the way in which God will purify the life of a nation. This indifference to holy things which is the way our age expresses itself can only be burnt out. Religion must cost us something if it is to have any purifying power. We must realize that God's touch, sometimes resting upon us with so gentle a caress, smoothing away our cares and sorrows may at other times, in Robert Louis Stevenson's great phrase 'stab our spirits broad awake'.

But be not dismayed at that—rather be dismayed if it tarries. For there is a cleansing ministry in the divine touch that hurts so much, and long after our hurt is healed our purified life will sweeten others by its gracious message.

CHAPTER V

A MAN ABSOLVED

'For I am the least of the Apostles, that am not meet to be called an Apostle.'

THIS is an amazing remark from one who, second only to Christ Himself, has been the greatest influence on the spiritual life of every generation that has come after him. This is astonishing humility: humility amounting to dismay.

But this man is not dismayed at the greatness of the task which faces him or at his own inadequacy for it. On the contrary, 'I can do all things,' he cries triumphantly, 'in him that strengtheneth me'. Nor does he need the re-assurance of divine fellowship. So real has that become that his ringing words come inspiringly across the years: 'Nothing shall be able to separate us from the love of God!'

Nor is he dismayed at having to stand alone. He knows all about that kind of thing. 'At my first defence,' he writes to young Timothy; 'no one took my part, but all forsook me.' Absolutely alone he stood also at Athens, without a single kindred spirit in the city, and held his ground. But in spite of that, he does not need to be reassured of human fellowship. Indeed, writing as a prisoner with a military guard, he sends the gayest of messages to his friends at Philippi, thanking God upon all his remembrance of them, thanking God for their fellowship—so real a thing it was to him.

Not even is he dismayed at the laxity of national religion. He is the great pioneer of international religion—the first man to take the world view. 'In Christ all things hold together' is his massive faith. Only if the world can get rid of Christ can life finally disintegrate and fall to pieces. But not even by murder could men get rid of Jesus. No grounds here, therefore, for dismay.

What then does dismay this gallant soul? Naught but his own utter unworthiness and the bewildering condescension of God: 'I am not meet to be called an Apostle—yet He appeared to me.' Not fit to be one whom Christ sent forth, yet he *is* sent forth. Only a great soul can be dismayed at the forgiveness of God and the confidence of God. Smaller men would bask in the dignity of the position—but not this man. The thought of the honour God has conferred upon him just breaks him down completely. A horrible picture flashes on to the screen of his memory—a circle of fierce, vindictive men surrounding one fearless follower of his Lord: stones flying—hideous gashes of wounds—the face of an angel (so it seemed to Paul now) bruised and torn and covered with blood—Stephen felled to the ground and battered into unconsciousness and death—and on the outskirts of the crowd himself, Paul, consenting to his death. Yet this same man, himself, sent forth to preach the same Lord as Stephen had called upon to pardon his murderers. Paul could never forget that.

Nor can he forget the men and women he has hunted and harried, pursued and haled off to prison for their faith in Jesus. Their faces come crowding back into his memory. Frightened faces, but sustained by a wonderful confidence throughout all his vindictive persecution of them. You could bully these people, but you could not break them. How their memory haunts him now: 'Not meet to be called an Apostle, because I persecuted the Church of God.'

Has he then no sense of divine forgiveness, this great soul struggling with his own sense of unworthiness? Does he not believe his own Gospel? Can he not credit that God has put all this black record behind His back for ever?

Of course he believes it. It is just because he believes it with all his soul that his sense of dismay sweeps over him. He has been forgiven so much that he cannot forgive himself.

Was it not Studdert Kennedy who once dreamed he stood before the Judgment Seat of Christ and heard his own record read out. And at the end of the sorry recital Jesus looked at him and said simply: 'Well?' And he made the answer any honest man would: 'Please, can I go to hell?'

The plain truth is that you just cannot realize what God has forgiven you without it breaking you all to pieces.

This noble sort of dismay has a very unworthy counterpart. Injustice overtakes us, or loss or sorrow, and we resent it as something we should not be called upon to endure. We have done nothing to merit such treatment at the hands of God. 'What have I done to deserve this?' We rail at God for the unfairness of His dealing with us. Well, that argument is a two-edged sword. If you are big enough to apply it consistently you will soon find yourself facing insoluble problems. You have been granted the quite inestimable privilege of being born in a free country—a country where freedom does really mean something. What have you done to deserve that? Just nothing at all: what could you do, anyhow? Obviously nothing; yet it has happened to you. Perhaps you were brought up in a good Christian home. What have you done to deserve that? Nothing. Perhaps you have a happy home of your own. What have you done to deserve that? Many a better man than you has missed it. What of the hosts of friends who persist in doing you kindness out of all reason? What of the joys of music and colour; of mountains and tumbling seas; of gardens and waving fields of corn; of books and quiet; of birds—the gull's effortless flight or the song of the thrush at eve; of the laughter of bairns or the wonderful fidelity in the eye of your dog? Oh, a host of lovely things—read again Rupert Brooke's 'Great Lover', then ask yourself 'What have I done to deserve all this?' If you are a man of any soul at all you will be finding yourself in the mind of Paul ere you are done. 'Not meet to be called an Apostle—yet He appeared to me.'

Dismay, this, of exalted sort. For it may lead you, as it did Paul, to realize that, unfit as you are to be sent forth on the Master's work, your very vision of Him is the only thing that equips you. If you are finding a sort of spiritual bolt-hole in the idea that speaking to others is not much in your line I would advise you to be very sure you are being quite honest. I do not suggest that you make yourself into Public Nuisance No. 1 by buttonholing people in the street and asking them about their souls. That kind of thing is not even intelligent, much less Christian. Remember you are to love the Lord your God with all your mind as well as with all your heart. But remember, too, St. Theresa's great word that Christ has no body now on earth but yours, no hands but yours, no feet but yours: yours are the eyes through which Christ's compassion is to look out to the world, yours are the feet with which He is to go about doing good, and yours are the hands with which He is to bless us now. So be sure of your honesty before you decide you are not cut out for this type of service. A sense of unworthiness may be as great an asset as a shallow cocksureness would be a handicap. The one awakens a sense of need which is always a healthy thing to happen in your spiritual life. Nothing is less likely to happen with the other. And, anyhow, there is no question as to which is the more fitting attitude under the kind but searching eye of Jesus.

There is a famous picture by the Austrian artist, Gabriel Max, known as 'St. Veronica's Handkerchief'. It depicts the head of Christ crowned with thorns. I first saw a cheap print of it in a shop window in a city street, and my curiosity was aroused by the fact that the eyes were closed. There was, beneath the print, an inscription in French which I was laboriously spelling out when, happening to glance back at the face, I found the eyes had opened. The effect upon me I shall never forget. It was just as if I had met the Master face to face—and I know how *I* felt at that moment under the steady scrutiny. Cocksureness was just miles away.

Of course I know it was a mere optical illusion. When I finished the French inscription I learnt all about it and how it had taken fourteen colours to produce the remarkable effect. I also learnt where the original was and what it was valued at and other completely unimportant trivialities about it. For me all that was of no interest whatever. I had learnt one big thing: what it feels like to stand unexpectedly in the presence of Jesus with no escape from those unwavering eyes.

Some day I shall have it to do again; so will you. And in that Presence you will know this nobility of dismay: 'Not meet to be called an Apostle.' But, please God, you will know also that amazing sense of equipment—'He appeared to me'. It is one of the great paradoxes of Christianity that the man who is sure of himself in the presence of Jesus is never adequate for the task Christ sets him. The man who *is* adequate is the one who is sure of his Lord.

CHAPTER VI

THE DEFEAT OF GOD

*'While I was with them, I kept them in thy name
which thou hast given me: and I guarded them, and
not one of them perished, but the son of perdition.'*

IN our glimpses at great souls in the grip of dismay we
have seen how God sets about counteracting its paralysing
effect. The man overpowered by his own pitiful ordinari-
ness is made aware of his immense resources; he who feels
abandoned and alone is made conscious of fellowship; the
true patriot, longing for the uplift of his nation's ideals, is
shown how acute suffering may be the only way to burn
out impurity and in the very challenge of such a message he
is stung into action; the soul completely broken by his
realization of God's forgiveness is inspired by the call to
service he feels unworthy to undertake.

All these dismayed folk, however, gave God a chance to
do something with them. They were willing to listen and,
listening, found that new interpretation of their handicap
which altered completely its character; that bracing element which enabled them to reach lofty heights of conduct
by determining their attitude to the opposition—the argument of the kite-string again.

Not everybody does this, however. There are those who
sink from dismay to hopelessness. They handicap God by
losing heart. Said the clear-sighted Percy Ainsworth on one
occasion: 'It is not our ignorance and clumsiness that
baffle the Almighty—it is our despair.' Before we leave
this study of dismayed people, therefore, it will not be

without its value to look at one who thus defeated God—if only to show by contrast what happens when a man is not willing to listen.

I have often wondered what would happen at a baptismal service if the minister, asking the father to 'Name this child,' received the startling request: 'Christen him Judas.' I have never known it happen, for the stupidest parents will draw the line somewhere. Yet it was once an honoured name: borne by one of the greatest military leaders the Jews ever had, borne by one of Christ's own brothers, borne by two of the twelve disciples. Pathetic comment on how it came to be so despised that even the Gospel writer feels it incumbent upon him to avoid doing an injury to an innocent man by pointedly differentiating —'Judas—not Iscariot'—lest some of its odium fall upon the wrong person.

The name has been tainted for nearly two thousand years. It has never been able to wash out the stain left by those thirty pieces of silver. It is not enough for the poor, tormented man, consumed with remorse and with rage in his heart, to hurl them back at the heads of the priests who made the bargain with him; their significance still clings to him like a foul miasma from some moral swamp. Small wonder—fancy selling Jesus for £4 16s.! It was but the price of a slave, but it was all the Son of God brought in that blackest of black markets. And even if one brings it up to date, with the £ worth about 8s., it is only about £12—not much for One whose shoe-latchet a great man counted himself unworthy to unloose.

One is reminded by contrast of the seven clansmen of Glen Moriston who hid their beloved Prince Charlie when a price of £30,000 was upon his head and not one was tempted by the siller. Bonnie Prince Charlie cuts but a poor figure alongside the Carpenter of Nazareth, but even allowing for the difference in money values between the two periods, the price of one leader as compared with the other is a significant comment on how we get things wrong. As £4 16s. is to £30,000, so is Jesus to the Gay Chevalier. Amazing—but there it is.

So that wretched £4 16s. stained a good name—for up till then it was as good a name as Jesus (Barabbas, you remember, was said to be named Jesus!)—and the stain has not faded with the years. That is why no child is ever christened Judas nowadays. It just isn't done and probably never will be again.

Yet that is a pity—for Iscariot too might have won out of his overwhelming dismay if he had only given Jesus a chance. There was a time when I thought that when he hanged himself it was the most gentlemanly thing we have any record of his doing. Perhaps at that moment of black despair Judas thought so too. I was wrong and so was he, for might not God have made something of a soul capable of such passionate condemnation of self? Moreover, since the essence of forgiveness is to restore the old relationship to what it was before the cursed action was ever committed, obviously to rush out and hang oneself is to make forgiveness quite impossible. It is still offered, but can no longer be accepted. The divine plan is frustrated at its most vital point. There is nothing very gentlemanly about that.

It is, perhaps, far too much to expect that Judas, torn by such a convulsion of feeling as surged through him when there dawned upon him the full realization of what he had done, should sit down quietly and think things out. Yet if he only had done so, what a marvel of redeeming grace might he have become! For he would have realized that, just as his worst self had led him to sell his Lord, so, strangely enough, it was his best self which was urging him to destroy himself. Remorse is never an attribute of our evil self. He might have realized, had he given himself time and given Jesus a chance, that his best self was still alive and potent though, in its despairing urge to suicide, quite mistaken. He might have reflected on how Jesus had trusted him ever since He had known him—this Jesus who knew what was in men. The very fact of his being chosen at all; of his being made the treasurer of the little group; of his being sent out with the rest, two by two, with power to cast out demons and heal diseases, at which he was apparently as successful as the rest; and—most significant of all—of Jesus, in the upper room, knowing what he planned to do, nevertheless actually aiding him to get out of the room alive when half a dozen of the other disciples, fiery tempered enough to have killed him if they had guessed what he was up to and armed with a couple of swords at that, would have leapt upon him like tigers had they known the truth—all these things he might have realized had he but given himself time for them to filter into his mind. Could such thoughts have failed to lead him out of despair and back into the company of Jesus even if all he could have done was to seek His forgiveness and die with Him? We, looking dispassionately at the situation at this distance of time, can see that it would have been the merest horse sense to let the forgiving and restoring grace of God function when nothing else could: it is doubtful whether we would have done any better than Judas had we been overwhelmed with scorching, searing remorse, as was he. It is no easy business to seek the forgiveness of a man whom you have betrayed to a dreadful death. And things become harder rather than easier if that forgiveness is immediately forthcoming when sought, for the magnanimity he displays only throws into more glaring relief your injury of one capable of such nobility. There is something to be admired about the man who, though pardoned, cannot forgive himself—but it is wrong all the same. He is keeping alive the very thing the other man, having forgiven, wants to forget. The old relationship is not restored.

'But how can it be?' he asks in desperation. 'Things cannot possibly be the same as if the wretched affair had never happened. It *has* happened and I cannot forget it.'

Well, that is true enough as far as it goes—but it stops far short of the length to which our wonderful God can go. Not even God can make you as if you had never sinned: you cannot be put back and run that section over again. But He can treat you as if you had never run off the rails; He can banish it from His remembrance for ever. Your part of the business is to accept that divine deletion and not spend your strength laboriously keeping in repair the barrier between you that God has broken down.

You are not likely, if you loathe the thing you have done as greatly as Judas did, to take God's forgiveness cheaply, as though it had not cost Him much. It is quite impossible for us to know what it costs God to forgive sin, for every sin destroys some plan of His and makes its fulfilment for ever impossible; every sin compels God to be content with a second best, for you cannot overtake the consequences of a sin by forgiving it. You are not likely to talk complacently about forgiveness being God's business—what He does for a living, so to speak—if you know remorse on the Iscariot scale. You are more likely to err at the other extreme. But you must give God a chance with you and in spite of your utter disgust at yourself you must focus your thinking upon His pardon and not upon your sin.

Not otherwise can your greatest handicap, your own wrongdoing, be changed in its character from a memory of evil that drags you down to a reminder of forgiveness that lifts you up.

Part Three

Reassurance

CHAPTER VII

GOD'S SECOND BEST

'The things which happened unto me have fallen out rather unto the progress of the gospel.'

WE have said that most of our reassurances come from realizing that our handicap is capable of an interpretation which changes its entire nature and changes therefore our entire reaction to it. We shall, I hope, see in due course, when we come to look at our spiritual equipment, that most of its valued elements could never have been ours at all had we never known frustration and loss and bereavement and disability and temptation and failure. But long before we start looking to our equipment—indeed, before we are even interested in possessing any—we need to be awakened to the fact that, no matter how crippled a life we feel to be living, we are far from being useless lumber. If we cannot carry out the task we had set our hearts upon, God is not at His wits' end to know what to do with us. He is the supreme artist at scheming and planning and improvization. Constantly being driven back upon a second best when His original plan is thwarted, He nevertheless produces something amazingly good. And He would have us too realize that that which is left for us to accomplish after our own disability and frustration have overtaken us may also be amazingly good. Only then do we become much interested in equipment for which we can now visualize a task. So we have first of all need of reassurance, and God sends it to us more often than not by awakening us to the surprising fact that new things have become possible to us because of our handicap which we could never have managed otherwise.

We are not easy to convince that this is so. When our minds are bitter at experiences hard to understand; when we are smarting under the shock of first realizing that our ambitions will never be realized and our dreams never come true; when we know at last that our purposes are broken off, we are not in the mood to listen to God.

'My God, my God—Why?' we cry when some tragic sorrow has come surging into life and in a moment everything is changed and never can be restored. There is not much level thinking behind the question, but you are not in the mood for level thinking when your little world has crashed about your ears and you stand amid the ruins. Why should this happen to you? It is not a very intelligent question, but it is a very human one.

How often, too, you have set your hand to some noble piece of work. How fine and uplifting it seemed to you at first—what an inspiration to be spending yourself in it! But you met with discouragement and indifference and apathy and ingratitude; your early comrades lost interest and left you to it. The joy and zest went out of the work, and, sick at heart, you gave it up. Again you are not, just then, in the mood to listen to God. You not only feel your fellow men have not appreciated your efforts, you feel that even God Himself might have backed you up a bit better. Even He seems to have left you to it without even showing Himself much interested. He sent you very little encouragement for your pains, anyhow. There is not much level thinking about that either, but when you are soured by disappointment you are not in the mood for level thinking.

We must all travel the hard road of failure and frustration at one time or another. If we struggle dourly on, undefeated, we often do so with little joy in our souls. We stick it out with a grim, dogged resolution, but it is a stern business with little laughter in it.

In such a sombre mood it will do us good to turn to what is, I think, the funniest story in the New Testament. It is, of course, written between the lines and must be pieced together with a sentence here and another there, and when you have read it you will no doubt say it is at least 90 per cent imagination and 10 per cent New Testament. It may be very near the truth for all that. In passing, it may be said that to read with a lively and instructed imagination is no bad method for making the Bible come alive to you. The story lies between two sentences in the letter to the Philippians: 'Now I would have you know, brethren, that the things which happened unto me have fallen out rather unto the progress of the gospel; so that my bonds became manifest in Christ throughout the whole praetorian guard and to all the rest.' And then, at the very end of the letter: 'All the saints salute you, especially they that are of Caesar's household.'

This amazing man seems positively to revel in his frustrations. He writes of them with almost a chuckle of amusement at their futility. It is difficult to realize he is writing from prison. Not from a prison dungeon certainly, for he was allowed to have his own house, but one has a shrewd suspicion it would not be much of a place. If the letter was written during his imprisonment in Rome—the traditional view—that great city was, in the first century, only about a third the size of the Leeds of today and about a million people were crowded into it. The people lived in houses ten or twelve stories high and rents were so enormous that we learn a census revealed the fact that there was an average of two or three families to each room. What sort of a lodging Paul would be able to afford in such circumstances, one can only imagine.

If, on the other hand, the letter was written during an

imprisonment in Ephesus, we know from Paul himself [1] that while he lived in that city he worked for his own living, and it seems reasonable that a working man, even if allowed to earn what he could during his imprisonment, would not have much to spend on rent. He was, moreover, chained by the wrist to a soldier—awkward enough for a manual worker, to say nothing of the exasperating complete lack of privacy.

Wherever he was, therefore, he is restricted and limited, fettered and confined. He is never without his guard, yet that soldier manacled to him—or that succession of soldiers, for one would relieve another—came to be a most important feature in the story. But of that more anon. We are, at the moment, more concerned with the man at the other end of the chain. By the time he had finished his course he had become somewhat used to chains. In fact, his biography reads more like a story from Alexander Dumas than from the New Testament. For nearly a quarter of a century he lives through one long, hectic record of thrilling adventure: his life is attempted—he makes a breath-taking escape in a basket—he is stoned by a hostile mob, tried for heresy, mobbed, arrested, imprisoned, liberated, mobbed again— what a business! He was a bonny fighter, however, and his dauntless spirit was not often cast down and never was utterly broken. Not even his two years' imprisonment at Caesarea—it took as long as that for Felix, the Roman Governor, to decide finally that this man would not buy his release with a bribe; his mind being, no doubt, made up for him when Paul exercised his rights as a Roman citizen and appealed to Caesar—not even that weary time subdued him. So to Rome he is sent—being, incidentally, ship-wrecked on the way just to keep things interesting, as it were—and there he waits another two years before his case is heard.

[1] Acts. 20. 34.

Here is frustration with a vengeance! Remember this man is the greatest preacher in the world—so great a leader of men that after nearly two thousand years he is still moulding the thought of the Christian Church; a dynamic personality with tremendous drive and initiative; a pioneer of the Kingdom of God under whose leadership many churches had been founded, the care and oversight of them still lying upon his heart. Who amongst us could have faced such intolerable and interminable interference without furious exasperation? Charles Dickens's 'Circumlocution Office' could teach Roman tyrants nothing in the art of wasting time, delaying justice, and exhausting patience.

Furthermore, for years he has been longing to visit Rome to preach there. When at long last he arrives, he is a prisoner and not allowed to preach. Tantalus, standing in his lake of water which receded from him whenever he stooped to drink, could know no greater teasing torment. What more natural than that the joy and zest should have gone out of life for Paul, thwarted and frustrated to such a degree? Yet, on the contrary, we find an amazing gaiety of spirit; something incredibly approaching amusement: 'The things which happened unto me have fallen out rather unto the progress of the gospel.'

For the purpose of our argument here it matters little whether he wrote from a prison in Ephesus or a prison in Rome: the only trifle of geography which concerns us about him at the moment is that he is located at one end of a chain with a soldier at the other. Thus we come back to the soldier.

'You must not tell us what the soldier said!' thundered the judge to Sam Weller in the trial of Bardell *v.* Pickwick; 'it isn't evidence!' I wish we knew what these particular soldiers said who guarded Paul throughout his imprisonment: it would, I imagine, be evidence of the most diverting character as to how there came to be saints in Caesar's household. Here we must, admittedly, read between the lines and with some sanctified imagination. Paul, not allowed to preach, was nevertheless permitted to receive visitors, and people from all over, rich and poor alike, came to talk with him on the things of the soul. The soldier had to listen whether he would or no. It is one thing to be riveted by a speaker, but quite another thing to be riveted *to* him. In the one case you want to stay and in the other you have to. What would you and I have given to hear the conversation of a man whose thought is as challenging after twenty centuries as it was to his contemporaries! The soldier lads of the Praetorian Guard had this immense privilege. Think of the majestic spiritual conceptions of the Epistles to the Colossians, the Ephesians, and the Philippians. They were dictated in these circumstances with a soldier lad shackled by the wrist, listening the while. Is it so wild a flight of fancy to imagine that a spell of duty on guard over this extraordinary prisoner came soon to be regarded as quite an interesting job? Need we be surprised that it was something to talk about off duty? And is it really very astonishing that soldier boys of the Guard should do a spot of sweethearting with servant-maids of the Palace and should tell of anything out of the ordinary in their monotonous lives? And if something of this sort is what did actually take place, we can easily see how the Gospel gains an entrance even into the very citadel of Caesar—and having got in, anything may happen. That remarkable things did in fact happen is testified by the presence of 'saints in Caesar's household'. What is behind this? Something more than the gossip of soldier lads and servant girls: for in some way or other, they must have realized that this preacher in chains had some secret which had revolutionized his life and could revolutionize theirs. Was there something in this man's gospel even for a slave? Were they, in the eyes of this man's God, really of some worth, who counted for so little in the sight of their masters? How came they to imagine that such a wonderful idea might be really true? A queer thing happened one day which may have started it—a visitor for Paul, one of the many who sought him out, but this one really was somewhat unusual. He stood there tongue-tied and embarrassed, ragged, dishevelled, obviously completely down and out. Perhaps he had not anticipated the presence of the soldier, for what he had to say was not easy and it would have been much less humiliating could he have seen Paul alone. There is no need to ask, however, for a private interview: the chain and the Guard only too patently make that out of the question. So he stands troubled in mind, disconcerted, confused. Paul looks at him enquiringly. So great an expert at understanding the human heart has no need to be told that here is a soul in acute distress. His very silence, abashed and perplexed, is eloquent. But Paul himself becomes disturbed, for the lad's face is strangely familiar. He cannot place him, but that they have met before Paul is quite certain.

'How came you here, lad?' he says at length. 'Where have I seen you before?'

'You were a friend of my master's,' whispers the youth.

'I have it—of course, you were a servant of my friend Philemon. You went by the name of 'Young Profitable'. What on earth are you doing here? And how is my friend your master? Well, I hope . . .' Paul's voice tails off into nothing: the lad's confusion was painful. 'There's something wrong here, sonny—something very far amiss. Why have you left Philemon? Why are you here? How did you get here anyhow? Come, lad, tell me all about it. How you knew I was here I can't imagine—but here you are and here I am. Tell me your story. Never mind my soldier friend here: I can't get away from him, but he can't get away from me either till his spell of duty is up—we've just got to put up with each other, but he's a decent lad and we have become quite good friends. Don't mind him: he won't split on you, whatever you've done. Tell me all about it.'

Haltingly, shamefacedly, Onesimus begins his sordid tale. No need to tell Paul what a fool he had been to run away from such a good master—and not only to desert, but to break faith and rob him too. But he had been given a responsible task; his master had entrusted him with money and he had proved unworthy of his trust. Then the wretched story of those anxious hunted days; the money soon gone; only odd jobs to pick up; always the dread of detection by someone who might recognize him; sleeping anywhere he could; his hand against everybody and everybody's hand against him. Making his way to the big city where he thought he would be safe—more easily lost, anyway—but finding what a poor thing was this destitute freedom compared with his well-fed and responsible service! Now he is at the end of his tether. He had quite accidentally heard where Paul was. In despair he runs the risk of approaching one whom he knew would recognize him. What had he better do?

All the time the soldier listens. 'You're for it, right enough!' he no doubt said to himself. Not much mercy in those days for a slave who broke service.

And all the time Paul too listens. And then, at length, the miserable recital comes to an end. The soldier is more than interested in how Paul will handle this little packet of trouble. One wonders what he thought of the first move —for Paul asks the lad to become his own servant for the time being. A delicate touch—for this friendless boy needs, above everything else just now, someone to believe in him. It is a curious fact that we are always more interested in people we do something for than in people who do something for us. Paul does not want to lose contact with him once it has been established: what better method of anchoring the boy to him than to restore his confidence by trusting him and to restore his self-respect by giving him once more a purpose in life?

And so for some time Onesimus became Paul's house-slave, and from time to time the soldier had opportunity to see for himself what value this new religion set upon a slave—and a dishonest one at that.

'Yes, you've dropped on your feet, my lad,' mused the soldier; 'and it looks to me as if you're going to get away with it. Provided, of course, the fellow at Colossae never finds you and Paul never gives you away. But if ever that happens, I'm sorry for you!'

There were, however, still more surprises in store for the soldier. One day on relieving his comrade he finds Paul's servant strangely agitated. Obviously something has happened while he has been off duty. It is soon apparent what it is. Paul is dictating a letter to one Timothy, who sits writing by his side. The letter is to Philemon: it is about Onesimus. He is sending the slave back to his old master, but—amazing thing!—the slave is willing to go. He is deeply moved, but not, apparently, afraid. Obviously Paul and he have talked it over and both are agreed. So Paul dictates, Timothy writes, Onesimus consents, and the soldier listens.

Extraordinary letter this. Begins normally enough by sending greetings and recalling the great hospitality so often shown to the Church by Philemon in days gone by. Talks about the contrast with his own present chain and then brings in this lad Onesimus. Actually rises (or sinks!) to the level of a pun on the boy's name. 'Young Profitable—though to you he has been more like a bad debt!' Talks of how useful, however, the boy has been to him during his imprisonment and how he has become 'part of my very self'—would like to have kept him, but that would not be right, since he must have Philemon's approval for that. So he sends him back asking that he be received (the soldier can scarcely believe his ears here) not as a slave but as a brother! Astonishing—but more yet: 'if he robbed you and is in your debt, charge it up to me—I will pay you in full.' Reminds Philemon he also is in debt—and to Paul himself: 'Do you not owe your very soul to me?' Is quite confident Philemon will do all he asks. Ends up with the usual sort of greetings.

The soldier gives it up: he can make nothing of this sort of thing; never met it before. This treatment to a slave—a runaway slave, a dishonest deserter! Not come across any religion in his time that stood for this sort of method of treating people. But it did seem to make a new man of the fellow—no doubt about the change in him from the first day when he came in, hopelessly down and out, compared with him now.

'What the soldier said isn't evidence.'

One wonders what he said to his comrades in the Guard; what he said to his sweetheart in the Palace kitchens; and, most of all, what he said to himself.

'Can this new religion make anything of *me*?'

If we but knew, I think we should find it evidence of the highest importance as to how there came to be saints in Caesar's household.

I have described this as the funniest tale in the New Testament. The humour of it lies in Nero imagining he could fetter the Gospel by chaining up the preacher, and the Gospel, in spite of him, getting into the very Palace. How true is the word of the old Psalmist: 'The kings of the earth rise up and the rulers take counsel together against the Lord and against His Anointed, saying, Let us break their bonds asunder and cast away their cords from us. He that sitteth in the heavens shall laugh: The Lord shall have them in derision.'

Is it not true that God is the supreme artist at improvization? His will for Paul was not a prison—that was the will of Paul's enemies. But Paul is given a reassurance by an interpretation of his handicap that changed its entire nature and his entire reaction to it. It is quite simple. God just sees to it that not Paul's imprisonment but the reason for it is the fact which strikes the imagination of the soldier boys and the servant-maids—and because it is the *reason* for his imprisonment which is emphasized they cannot think of his chain and the thought of Jesus be far away. God's second best can be astonishingly good.

So also may be yours. But you must be a big enough soul to seek to interpret your handicap and not let yourself become the sport of it. You must lay hold of that steadying, bracing element which can make you face it squarely and resist it unwaveringly. Then you can climb.

CHAPTER VIII

EXPERIENCE AND EXPERIMENT

'I have yet many things to say unto you'

THESE two words spring from the same root, the Latin *experior*, to try, to prove, to pass through. They have come to mean such different things it is significant they start out from the same source. That fact alone is enough to set us thinking and may lead us a step farther in our exploration of the ways of God with us, and how He leads us from dismay to reassurance.

We have seen how He rekindles within us a sense of purpose when we had almost lost heart, bringing us to a belief in what may be a very wonderful second best. Obviously the next thing to do with us is to set us experimenting again that we may find out what is still possible. Experience is, after all, only the observed result of experiment. You take a note of what happens in certain circumstances and under certain conditions. You observe that whenever the circumstances are the same the results are the same. You make your experiments and build up your experience at the same time.

A friend of mine once took me into a large steel-works, where I witnessed the finest firework display I ever saw in my life. We went up into a small glass-sided cabin which looked out upon a huge flame roaring and blazing up into the air a few yards away. In the cabin I saw a man gazing intently at the flame and apparently doing nothing else. He took not the slightest interest in our arrival, never moving his gaze from the enormous tongue of fire.

'What's this man doing?' I asked, and my friend explained. He was watching the flame change colour. When it reached a particular tint he would give a signal, for the metal would then be exactly ready and would be poured out. I stood watching him as he, in turn, watched the flame. The change in colour had no significance to me: it meant something of supreme importance to him. The moment arrived: the signal was given; slowly the large ladle swung and tipped over and the white-hot liquid metal poured into the containers. I was back, for a moment, in my schooldays wondering what Guy Fawkes would have thought about this little lot. The finest rockets and roman-candles and catherine-wheels and what not faded into insignificance. I enjoyed it immensely. It was later on I fell a-wondering how much patient labour, how much financial loss, how much sickening failure, how much persistent endeavour, how much dogged defiance of discouragement went to the proving that the particular tint of the flame indicated the crucial moment in the preparation of the steel. There was a time when they did not know that; there was a time when they suspected it; there was a time when they thought it was so—and all the while they kept on experimenting and observing and noticing and learning. Now they no longer merely suspect or think—they know. Experience has been built up out of experiment. Certainty has grown out of belief.

We must be stimulated into this kind of thing in our spiritual life when once we have been lifted out of our dismay. The very reassurance we have been given is part of our experience, but we must realize the serious danger of separating experience and experiment. We must have experiment to achieve experience, but it is vital that we make our experience the starting-point for further experiment. Otherwise we are in danger of stagnating and limiting all growth in our souls.

It is curious how quickly we are apt to swing from one extreme to another. Faced with immense difficulties we lose heart and give it up: given a little encouragement we become too easily content, and, filled with a sense of accomplishment, we glow with satisfaction. It is a dangerous drug. We set our own limit to spiritual progress if we set ourselves a mark we can reach. It has been well, if somewhat cynically, said that 'Success is the penalty imposed on a man who has aimed too low'.

I once knew a boy who worked his way through quite a succession of hobbies. Something would interest him and for a while he was utterly absorbed in it. Then, having mastered it, he lost all interest in it and completely dropped it. Another subject would fascinate him and again he would work at it with all his energy, until, again, he exhausted and abandoned it. One thing after another held his attention only until it ceased to extend him, and then he would once more cast round for something else.

At length his mother got somewhat worried. Did this indicate an unstable character in her son, that he must flit from one thing to another, butterfly fashion, with no definite sustained, settled purpose? She consulted a wise friend. 'Set him on with music,' she was advised; 'he'll never get to the end of that!'

Much sound sense there was in that. One might think, at first glance, that to master a subject, to realize an ambition, to accomplish a purpose would have been such a satisfying experience that one could sit down and be happy ever after; but it does not work out that way. Curiously enough, it is the mark that is always beyond you which continues to inspire you. Not the one you reach, but the one you do not reach.

So the strange fact emerges that God takes hold of us in our days of dismay, reassures us by giving us a new slant upon our handicap, and straight away faces us again with a mark which is for ever beyond our grasp. Why is it, then, that we do not at once relapse into despair?

The answer is quite simple. We were dismayed by a problem or a task or a handicap which paralysed us by its greatness. We are taken into the presence of a Person who inspires us by His greatness. One reason, at any rate, why Jesus, generation after generation, continues to fascinate men is that you can never exhaust Him. He has always something fresh to say; always something new to teach; always something more with which to challenge you, towards which to lead you.

Fortunate it is for us that it is so. For life is infinitely more complicated today than ever it was before, and gives no indication of ever becoming simpler. Contrast your own life with the kind of existence enjoyed by the first disciples. They lived in the leisurely and contemplative East—we in the hustling, bustling West. In their day a man could not travel more quickly than a horse could carry him. Now the whole world has, in effect, shrunk in view of the immense speed with which we can get about. Then swords and spears, bows and arrows, primitive catapults and battering-rams were their weapons. Now we have in our hands such appalling power that for the first time in history mankind has the ability to commit race-suicide.

Obviously, then, if *all* that Jesus had to say could have been assimilated by such men as His first disciples with their comparatively simple problems, what use could He possibly have been to us with our far more complex lives, our far more intricate perplexities, our far more subtle temptations?

But we find Him telling those simple souls who first followed Him that He had many things to say to them, but they could not take them in, could not grasp their significance, could not appreciate their import. Fortunate for us, I say, that that was so. For if He was so infinitely more than adequate for them, therein lies our hope that He is likely to be adequate for us too. No more convincing proof could be given that Jesus is, indeed, the Son of God than the fact that age after age, in spite of life's progressive complexity, He remains the great final moral authority. Like my friend who never got to the end of music, we never reach the point when we have left Jesus behind.

It is of course the merest platitude—what *Punch* would call another glimpse of the obvious—to say that every age needs a final moral authority; but this age stands in greater need than probably any before it. No previous generation has had, at one and the same time, such complete education in organized devilry and such incredible facilities for applying it. No previous generation has had such power of devastation and consequently such temptation to use it. Does anybody know how this immense capacity for evil is to be controlled? We have need to listen to this same Jesus, who said to men two thousand years ago: 'I have yet many things to say unto you.' There is little doubt His word to us is likely to be the same.

He does, at any rate, challenge us to make our experience *of* Him the starting-point of further experiment *with* Him. We are, in fact, challenged from both sides in our present dilemma. The very possession of such power as science has now given us constitutes a moral problem of the first magnitude. 'Live under God or live underground' is a cynicism with far more truth in it than one generally finds in the wit of cynics. It is the challenge of the very facts which face us; but it is also the challenge of the crucified Carpenter who alone knows how to handle such inflammable stuff without heading straight for disaster. The blunt truth is that the only adequate answer to atomic power is a revival of religion and only those who have the courage to listen to Jesus Christ can have anything to say worth serious attention. This is not to argue that because a man is a

Christian therefore he is automatically equipped to handle immense international problems. That would be too absurd for anything. A man is not necessarily a statesman because he is a Christian. It is, however, to argue, and to argue very emphatically, that if he is gifted as a statesman at all, he will be a better statesman if he is a Christian than if he is not. To keep politics out of religion is generally good sense, but to keep religion out of politics is sheer lunacy, for it is deliberately to jettison the most valuable cargo of the ship of state: its moral standards, which are a matter of religion and cannot spring from any other source. It does, however, take a deal of courage to take Christ so completely at His word that you are prepared to accept His control of affairs.

Jesus once told an interesting little story about a business man who was going abroad. He was a shrewd old boy and called in the members of his staff, one by one, before he set out, and allocated certain of his interests to them to attend to during his absence. He had each of them fairly accurately measured up and each man was given sufficient responsibility to extend his energies and his initiative. Then off he went and left them to it.

On his return he called for their reports, and those who had done well he rewarded—and, to my mind, the touch of the artist in the story lies in the rewards this astute merchant gave. 'Well done, good and faithful servant . . . now you can retire on pension.' Nothing at all like that. The reward of a good job well done is a bigger job to do—not less responsibility but more. 'Faithful over a few things, I will make you ruler over many.'

We love to reflect upon that tale as our Lord's own picture of how God treats men. It is, however, equally striking (though admittedly this was not Christ's point in telling the story) as an illustration of how Jesus invites us to treat Him. 'Believe me for the very works' sake,' He cries, apparently quite content that we should try Him out and find for ourselves that He can make good His claim that He will never let us down. And, indeed, if we will but venture to entrust our interests to Him, He is quite prepared to stand by the result. It is something of a staggering thought that He is prepared to be treated as a wise business man treats his staff—trusting them with increasing responsibility as they prove capable of handling it. Each venture the merchant makes is an experiment on his part—each fulfilment his servant accomplishes builds up his employer's experience of the man. So the merchant entrusts larger and larger issues to the servant and every time he rises to the occasion his master's confidence in him is deepened. The final test is when he will make the experiment of entrusting not his business interests but his life to another. The man who must serve him in that crisis is trusted indeed. Jesus asks for nothing better. 'I am among you as he that serveth,' He says. 'Let me win your confidence. Make your experiments; build up your experience. Give me the chance: that is all I ask.'

Many years ago I heard a story which greatly thrilled me. I wish I could remember who told it that I might make due acknowledgement of my debt, but that has gone from me. The adventure befell a group of friends climbing in the Alps and making their dangerous way along a narrow ledge on the rock face with a sheer wall on one side and a sheer drop on the other. They were led by an experienced guide, the only one of the party who had previously made the ascent. They reached a point where this narrow ledge turned a sharp corner, and they found to their dismay that at that critical point some recent fall of rock had demolished the path. By a piece of superb mountaineering the guide managed to negotiate the corner and swing himself on to the path beyond the break. With the skilful use of the rope the next one or two followed. Then the crisis happened—the next man lost his nerve. Half the party round the corner; half still to come; and a man sobbing with fright in the middle. The guide ordered the men on his side of the corner to lie flat while he walked over their bodies back to the broken ledge. Then he lay flat himself and reached out round the corner a strong, sinewy arm and outstretched palm. Then, speaking quite calmly to the unnerved climber, he said: 'Place your foot on my hand and walk round. That hand never yet lost a man.' Only confidence like that can beget confidence sufficient for such an ordeal. It was a great experiment; it led to a great experience.

The whole of mankind stands today at a very awkward corner. The old paths are broken. We must trust to a Person. I believe Christ can get us round if we have the courage to entrust the future destinies of the race to Him. But that is an experiment none of us is able to make, for none of us can speak for the race as a whole. I believe He can get us round if we have the courage to entrust the future destinies of the nation to Him. But that is an experiment few of us can make, for not many of us speak for the nation. I believe He can get us round if we each have the courage to trust ourself to Him—and that is an experiment you *can* make. He will not let you down. His hand never yet lost a man. He is not baffled by our dilemma, as we are. On the contrary, 'I have yet many things to say unto you', He says. I suggest He is worth a hearing.

CHAPTER IX

HOW TO FIND OUT THE WILL OF GOD

'If any man willeth to do his will he shall know . . .'

THE Gospels are full of stories of people who made experiments and gained experience, and not the least interesting is of Jesus sending out the twelve, two by two, to preach, to heal the sick, and to subdue unclean spirits. He seems to have been very particular in teaching them how to behave when they were guests in somebody's home—a shrewd touch, for you generally remember a gracious presence long after you have forgotten a good sermon.

There is one curious feature, however, which, as this is a book primarily for handicapped people, is of immediate interest to us. Jesus sends them out deliberately handicapped. The one thing He apparently will not have on any consideration as a characteristic of His disciples is independence. He equips them with subtractions. 'Don't take any money; don't take any food wallet; don't take two pairs of shoes; don't cumber yourself with two coats.' A commissariat of minus quantities. Truly men do need a positively reckless faith to do what Jesus suggests. They did then—they do now. God seems to delight throughout all the ages in choosing the foolish things, the weak things, the base things, the despised things to bring to nought the things that are strong.

But this was no mere whimsicality on the part of Jesus. There is point in this divine handicap, as there always is. It is not an absence of equipment—it is part of their equipment. Jesus would have His disciples aim not only at being helpful people, but also at being people capable of being helped. He would have us avoid being too obviously self-sufficient. People are not often attracted by those who are blatantly able to look after number one. They generally leave them to it. On the other hand, as we have already seen, they are always more interested in people they serve than in people who serve them. That is why there is more spiritual genius in getting five men to help you than in doing the work of six men yourself. We all smile at the well known story of the Irish inventor who constructed a machine to do the work of ten men but it took twelve men to work it. But in the world of the spirit that is as intelligent as in the world of industry it is absurd: you have two more people interested in the job in hand.

Anyhow the disciples came back from their experiment and they had to admit the scheme worked. Said Jesus (I am sure with a twinkle in His eye): 'When I sent you forth without purse and wallet and shoes, lacked ye anything?' And they said, 'Nothing!'

It is quite evident, therefore, that there are things we would count essential to our Christian work which Jesus sets very little store upon. But there is one thing that we often lose sight of altogether which in Christ's eyes is absolutely vital. The essential thing for these men, as for the seventy who followed them, was their sense of commission; the constant remembrance of what they were after; of who sent them; of Jesus Himself being with them. 'When *I* sent you out,' said Jesus, 'ye lacked nothing.'

It would have been a highly entertaining story to have listened in to their comments one to another when they were first briefed for this adventure. They were being sent out on work they had never done before, work they had seen Jesus do, but which they had not tried their hands at with any success. Now they were given the job to do. Peter, doubtless, had no lack of confidence, but what about Philip, for instance? He was good at arithmetic, but quite a novice at casting out devils. Or Thomas, with his legal mind, wanting evidence and weighing probabilities—what did he think of the prospects? Or Bartholomew, that somewhat shadowy figure of whom we know so little? Many of us have chuckled with a certain measure of sympathy at Rob Dow in Barrie's *Little Minister*, who taught his son to learn the names of the Apostles from Luke sixth, but said, 'Miss out Bartholomew, for he did little, and put Gavin Dishart in his place.' What did Bartholomew, this man who has left so little a mark on the Gospel page, think about the great experiment? Or Judas? Deep, unfathomable man with a queer twist in his nature which worked out to such a tragic end: the treasurer whose accounts did not balance, yet who was now called upon to employ in the healing of the sick those same hands which pilfered from the funds. Did his call set him wondering whether Jesus didn't know all about him, after all, for surely He would not have commissioned a rogue to cast out devils after all He had said about Satan being divided against himself!

Or Simon the Zealot—fierce political extremist that he was—what did he think? A strange method this of establishing a kingdom—preaching and healing and being dependent on others—not *his* idea of how it should be done: no organization, no troops, no funds, no plan, no anything.

With very mixed feelings they must have set out—but they came back thrilled by their experience.

'Lacked ye anything?' 'Nothing.'

However absurd, however impossible might seem the task, they knew who had sent them and their sense of His being behind them in everything gave them a confidence which nothing could daunt. They were surprised at themselves: surprised and exhilarated—as we would be if we worked at our own tasks with the same sense of commission; the same certainty of being busy with a divinely appointed purpose, of having Christ behind us in all we undertook.

'Ah,' but you say, 'that's just the rub. These men had no doubt of being on Christ's work because He actually in person sent them out. We have no such simplifying element in our work for God. On the contrary, our whole problem is how to be sure that the task we are asked to do is really His design for us. The invitation often comes from such an unlikely source and in such unimpressive circumstances. How are we to know the hand of God is in it?'

That is quite a fair question. How can a man learn what is the will of God for *him*? It is certain that a great host of homely, honest-to-goodness, plain, ordinary folk would give much to know. They feel that the whole business is mysterious and that nobody who is not half a mystic has much chance of finding anything definite in it. They are not mystics and feel completely out of their depth in consequence. Profound and abstruse theories leave them rather cold, for they are not profound or abstruse thinkers and do not profess to be. Moreover, they feel—with a good deal of reason—that God might have made some provision for the needs of plain, simple people who would willingly do His will if they knew what it was. After all, if Jesus could teach the divine will with such simplicity that the common people heard Him gladly, finding themselves neither bored nor bewildered, it seems a pity if God has lost the knack.

That God has not lost the knack is proved quite conclusively by the number of very homely people who *have* found their niche and fill it with a great content. Their simple tasks are carried out without ostentation and without parade but with a complete certainty that they are where God wants them to be and that if the Master suddenly appeared to them they would have no need to apologize for what He found them busy with. 'Courage, gaiety, and the quiet mind,' in Robert Louis Stevenson's unforgettable phrase, are their normal atmosphere. How is this manner of living achieved? There must be some quite simple method of winning through to it or they could never have done it.

What immediately follows is not for the seers or the saints; not for those of deep spiritual insight and culture: not for the men and women 'far ben' with their Lord, as the lovely old Scots phrase has it. Rather is it for those who have to live out their lives in a setting of practical duties which do not minister to quiet reflection. A busy common-sense atmosphere is their native air, where if certain things are neglected, other things go wrong: where if you fail to pull the lever, the cogs do not engage, where if you do not use your intelligence, things kick back at you later on. Thus the normal bent of their minds has in it nothing of the mystical, much of the practical. For all such who would set about finding out God's will in their characteristic horse-sense way, the following homely approach is suggested.

Before you make a telephone call you have already decided (perhaps quite unconsciously) three things: that there is somebody at the other end (for the sake of the illustration we will rule out 'no reply'); that he will be able to understand what you say; and that you will be equally able to understand him. Otherwise there is no point in ringing up. You must make up your mind upon the same three things in speaking to God—and, again, you will be well advised to rule out 'no reply,' for you will always get one—always.

Begin by accepting the fact, therefore, that you are dealing with a God who can make Himself understood by ordinary people and that you have within yourself the power to interpret the language of God.

Then go on to remind yourself of a truth we have already noticed in a previous chapter, that God is at any rate reason-ably intelligent and expects you to be the same. This implies, on His part, that if He has a work for you to do He will make it not only possible but comparatively simple for you to learn what it is. Anything short of this would be rather senseless. On your part is implied that you will be prepared to go to some trouble, nevertheless, to discover it, that you will not expect to have all your thinking done for you. This is what Jesus meant by 'loving the Lord thy God with all thy mind'.

Go still further and refresh your mind about something more we have already learnt, that the work God designs for you, whatever it is, is something you can do *if you try*. When you do learn what it is you may find that its importance may take your breath away. Never mind. Remember what you have just decided about God's intelligence and reflect for a moment on what on earth would be the use of setting you a task you could not possibly bring to success. You will soon come to see in the magnitude of the task God's conception of how much you are to be trusted with. You cannot rely too greatly on the intelligence of God.

All this is such simple common-sense stuff that it may be thought too childishly trivial to waste time stating it at all, especially as we are deliberately going over the ground a second time, yet it is not without value to convince ourselves that we do not need a special type of mind, nor a lengthy training by some expert, to begin to talk to our Father. God has always far more bother with those who think it difficult than with those who think it natural. That is why Jesus placed a mischievous laddie in the midst of a company of solemn adults, telling them to keep their eye on him and do their best. Let us believe quite definitely that it is *not* difficult to learn the will of God. How then do we set about it?

Some years ago I found myself on an oil-tanker sailing down the east coast of North America from Virginia to the Mexican Gulf. We kept so close to the shore that we could actually see people having picnics on the beach. Curious as to the reason for our hugging the coast in this fashion, I enquired why it was.

'The Gulf Stream is against us,' I was told; 'we are keeping inshore to keep out of the current.'

On the return journey, however, we launched far out to sea and there was added to the pulse of our own engines the mighty urge of that tremendous flow. It was no longer our purpose to keep out of the stream, but to get into it. So were we borne along by a power extra to and infinitely greater than our own. The important thing was first to know the direction of that power and then to join up with it. Which is something of a parable.

Hear another: The worried little man climbed on to the table in the operating theatre. 'Doctor,' he said anxiously: 'I've a wife and six bairns. You'll do your best for me?' The surgeon was one of the greatest in the land. He smiled encouragingly. 'Money cannot buy my second best,' he said. Which is also something of a parable.

Hear a third: 'I have just met a great man,' announced wee Jimmy, aged six. 'And how do you know he was a great man?' asked his mother, not realizing he only meant 'big.' 'He *was* a great man, mummy: he had to stoop such a long way to talk to me.'

In those three homely and quite disconnected incidents there lie three fundamental principles for finding out the will of God. There is in the affairs of men in this distracted world of ours a stream of kindly and beneficent works. It is good to remind ourselves of its existence when we become depressed at the spate of devilry which has been let loose in our time ; good to reflect that there are millions of generous acts and helpful agencies and uplifting movements constantly operating all around us. They are not so spectacular as the evil things and do not make such good stories for the newspapers and, perhaps for this reason, it is not always easy to preserve a sense of proportion and to keep things in proper perspective. Not all of these good causes are connected with the Churches, though every one of them springs from the Church if you go far enough back into origins. But, whether or not you have any use for Churches, if you will study the direction of this powerful current of kindly impulse you will find it is all towards the uplift of your fellow men; towards the improvement of conditions of life in every department; and, above all, towards the change of heart and mind, loyalties, and thinking of every one of us. Get into the stream of good works: do something for nothing: go to some trouble for others without expecting any reward: remember Wordsworth's searching word that

> *high Heaven rejects the lore*
> *Of nicely-calculated less or more.*

You will not be long at this sort of thing without finding an immense satisfaction in the work itself, quite apart from the friendships you will make and the happiness you will create. And what is more important, sooner or later there will come to you an insistent, persistent voice: 'This is your work—this is your work—this is your work.' When you hear it, for God's sake and for your own soul's sake listen. It is the voice of God to you.

You will learn, ere long, that the will of God for you is an exacting business. If you are in your prime and glorying in your fitness, it will make you go all the distance; if you are crippled and handicapped it will be adapted to your powers, but it will still extend you. You must always do your best for your fellows. Your second best is never good enough—it should never be in the market. God has so arranged that the great surgeon and the charwoman can both enjoy the pride of the craftsman. 'All service ranks the same with God' sings Robert Browning, and we are grateful for the reminder. It is, however, only true of the best you have to offer in whatever sphere you labour. Your second best may be much better than my best, but that is not the point. You will find, as the will of God becomes clearer to you, it will call ever for the highest you can rise to.

And paradoxically enough—for the lowest you can stoop to. We often use the phrase of 'stooping to an unworthy action', but there is a sense in which we stoop to a gracious one. Is not true greatness always measured by its stoop? Can you measure God in any other way? Or the children of God?

What withering satire Jesus poured out upon those who think themselves great because they can lord it over others. God seldom appoints representatives who know how to strut but not how to stoop. We really are dreadfully slow in the uptake in these matters: if a man bellows loudly enough we still rush to do his bidding, whereas if he stoops to our level that he may help us to rise to his we generally recognize his greatness after he is dead.

Jesus has defined the great man, and His definition will last for all time: he is a Servant. You just cannot be great unless you are a servant. There is in Christ's eyes only one justification for a person employing servants and that is that he himself is thus liberated for more important service which less gifted people could not do.

Into this mighty current of beneficent and helpful ministry therefore launch yourself. It will not be long before you learn God's will for you.

CHAPTER X

KINDRED SPIRITS

'No longer do I call you servants; for the servant knoweth not what his lord doeth: but I have called you friends.'

MOST of us have had the experience of climbing, inspired constantly by the vision of the summit ahead of us, and of finding when we approached the top that the real peak came into view far, far ahead and that we have been toiling up only a shoulder of the mountain.

Jesus is rather like that. We think we know His mind after long and arduous study—and immediately we catch a glimpse of some further height far beyond our present achievement. We have reached such a point now. We have just found Him telling us that the foundation of all greatness is to be a servant. And no sooner have we grasped that fact than we find Him telling us that to be a servant is really a very little thing and that He wants us to go considerably higher than that. There can be something very fine and something very paltry about obedience: something very soul-uplifting and something very soul-destroying. There is a kind of service which kills all the creative urge, all the artist element in a man, dulls him and humiliates him until he is a mere cog in a wheel and his work is drained of all interest and fascination. We have all heard of the type of employer or official or foreman—any 'proud man drest in a little brief authority'—who pompously snubs his work-man, informing him, 'You are not here to think, you are here to do what you are told', and thereby fondly imagines he exhibits his own outstanding superiority. No man is really great who makes another feel small, and this kind of fool may well be left to his folly. He enjoys his own importance and may as well die happy without realizing how few share his opinion.

But sometimes it is not the master but the work itself which drains away all initiative. I knew a man who worked for eighteen months in Ford's motor works in Detroit on 'Nut 22'. He left in order to preserve his sanity and self-respect. 'I found it a deadening and degrading occupation,' he told me. He had no illusions about his own ability: he did not imagine himself another Henry Ford merely lacking opportunity; but never to visualize his master's design; never to be given any breadth of outlook; never to see anything growing under his hand; never to be *building* anything, but merely to be making a tiny insignificant bit of a complicated machine, which machine by its very complexity was a thing of beauty to an engineer—to be condemned to a narrow, unintelligent obedience became completely intolerable. He had to clear out or go mad. One wonders how much of the old spirit of craftsmanship modern methods of mass production have destroyed.

Nevertheless, even unintelligent obedience can rise on occasion to splendid heights. A great deal of military discipline is built upon it. 'Their's not to reason why, Their's but to do and die'—even though someone had blundered and the most tom-fool instructions were the result. That sort of thing can be magnificent when, in a crisis, the will of one person must be unhesitatingly accepted, no matter how absurd it may seem, if utter confusion is not to ensue.

But to extend beyond the critical situation the demand for that kind of obedience is to sink into dictatorship on the one hand and bondage on the other. Nothing could be further from the attitude of Jesus towards us nor the response He desires from us. He certainly wants implicit and immediate obedience from us, even to the death—and the astonishing thing about Him is that in every generation He has received it; but He never dragoons men and never makes slaves of them. Paul, it is true, gloried in the phrase 'the bondservant of Christ', but nothing less like slavery can be imagined than the service of that great man to his Lord.

Which leads us inevitably to the real crux of the matter: the quality of service reveals not only the character of the servant but, probably even more, the character of the Master. And that is why there is no inconsistency in Jesus regarding service as the bedrock of greatness and immediately going on to say He does not want us as servants. We see at once what Jesus really wants from us when we put His words and Paul's alongside each other.

'No longer do I call you servants,' says Jesus, 'for the servant knoweth not what his lord doeth: but I have called you friends; for all things that I heard from my Father I have made known unto you.'

'Have this mind in you,' says Paul, 'which was also in Christ Jesus.'

Once learn to think as Jesus thinks and you will no longer offer Him that type of discipleship which cannot aim any higher than merely doing what it is told: which has to have all its thinking done for it and cannot see in Christianity anything more than 'playing the game' or refraining from those things which are 'not done' and, in general, being a decent sort of fellow. 'Give me friendship, not service,' cries Jesus; 'give me the intelligent insight into my purposes that I have the right to expect from a kindred spirit. Get away from the little niggling trivialities which can so easily form a large part of your religious life unless you learn to think as God thinks.'

Most of us fall under this reproof. It is so easy to lose

one's sense of proportion, so easy to magnify details so that they become invested with an altogether ludicrous importance, so easy to be blind to the good in a man who thinks differently from ourselves, so easy to refuse to co-operate when we receive what we regard as inadequate recognition.

One thinks of the MacDonalds at Culloden who would not fight because they were not allocated the position in the line of battle which they regarded as the right of their great clan. I was pulling the leg of a friend of mine of that name about this very incident. 'Ah,' he replied, 'true enough—but see what happens when the *MacDonalds* refuse to fecht! The battle's lost, man!' Which was a witty evasion of the point. It is not much use proudly drawing attention to the chaos which results when we, with all our importance, stand aloof. The real moral of the incident is the chaos which results when we lose our sense of proportion. And, let me repeat, most of us fall under this reproof, for unintelligent discipleship so often concentrates on a detail and fails to visualize the whole design. 'Nut 22' again —though this time by the choice of the worker, not of the Master, which is an even worse tragedy.

I had a friend who was at one time attached to the British Legation in a foreign capital. His chief was a very remarkable man, of great personality as well as great ability. Working in close touch with him, my friend came to know his mental processes so well that in time he found he could, so to speak, project himself into the mind of his chief so that when he was left to carry on in his leader's absence he came to be able to decide without much difficulty what he should do by imagining what his chief would do. That was, in a very real sense, 'having the mind in you which was in another'. Here was no blind obedience but the co-operation which comes of thinking alike. Here was no 'doing what you are told', for he wasn't told anything, but rather the instinctive parallel reaction of a kindred spirit. That is the kind of thing Jesus wants.

How unthinkingly we pray daily, 'Thy will be done in earth as it is in heaven', yet if we would only pause and reflect a moment, instead of allowing familiarity to drain that tremendous prayer of all meaning, we would be amazed at its implications. True, all nature fulfils the will of God— every blade of corn that ripens to the ear, bringing forth thirty-fold, sixty-fold, a hundred-fold; every bird of the air that takes its quota and pays for it in service or in song; every beast of the field, every fish of the sea fulfils its divine function; but obviously, since mankind is the pinnacle of God's creation, only by mankind can God's finest will be done on earth. His finest will is a thing of the spirit, for which reason He has taken us into His confidence, explaining to us the great purposes in which we are given a part, not condemning us to a dull and deadening following of the rules.

It was said of Schubert that his was a soul so full of melody that he would jot down on the backs of old envelopes, or any scrap of paper he found to his hand, themes which danced into his mind—and perhaps a week or so after would find one of them lying about, would pick it up and hum it over, exclaiming, 'That's a pretty tune! I wonder who wrote it?' quite unconscious of the fact he had written it himself. You cannot reach that sort of level merely by knowing and observing the rules of harmony and counterpoint: it is the very essence of music—a thing of the spirit, not of the law.

We have been called upon to live in an age which thinks very little of Churches but which, paradoxically enough, has a very keen sense of the spirit of Christ whenever it sees it exhibited. It has an even keener sense of resentment at being fobbed off with something inferior where it expects to find the genuine article. As in the instance, for example, of a holiday-maker who, one Sunday afternoon, casually entered a little Methodist Chapel some years ago and had the misfortune to listen to a preacher whose spiritual horizon was entirely bounded by the four walls and the roof of his own little Bethel. And when at last the tormented worshipper staggered out into God's sunshine again he was heard to exclaim: 'To hear that man talk you would think God was a Wesleyan!'

No one who had accepted Christ's offer of this new relationship—friends not servants—could ever have preached a sermon like that: without range of vision, or breadth of scope, or depth of purpose, or height of ambition. One wonders what sort of a little god (not worthy even of a capital G) such a preacher served. It is significant with what promptitude even a casual worshipper rejected the counterfeit. And, after all, he was only echoing the protest of Jesus Himself. Very far indeed from possessing the mind of the Master is he who would crush God into his own mould and strive to make Him fit the confines of his own petty notions.

Yet how reassuring—to return at long last to our real subject—it is to find Christ taking it for granted that we have it in us to rise to a level so much above the servant mind: and not only taking it for granted that we *can*, but that at any rate some of us *will* rise to it. Here is confidence on the grand scale. Surely He must be the most hopelessly deceived or the most far-seeing person to credit us with such inherent possibility. But we cannot believe Him deceived without writing ourselves off as much poorer creatures than He conceives us to be, nor can we believe Him far-seeing without catching the inspiration of His faith in us. And when any soul, handicapped and discouraged, realizes that he may still be a kindred spirit with his Creator and his Redeemer, it is small wonder that life takes on a fresh radiance. Thereafter, with this reassurance

taking possession of him, a handicap becomes an opportunity and by it he is equipped for greater service.

So it was with Brother Willie. Thus he was affectionately
known to a great host of folk who came to thank God they
ever met him. He was, without doubt, one of God's elect.
His gift—as definitely a gift of God as ever was preacher's
eloquence or poet's vision—was fun. He was the greatest
genius at making people friendly that ever I met. He was
the most expert 'ice-breaker' I have known. He could
walk into a room where he knew nobody and nobody
knew anybody else; where, with true English reserve and
stupidity, nobody had anything to say and all were pro-
foundly uncomfortable, and in five minutes he would have
them all talking as freely as if they were at a reunion. He
could keep a company in high good humour by telling the
most absurd tales, at which you laughed uproariously even
though you had heard them fifty times before. Then,
sometimes, with no sense of incongruity at all, he would
finish up by taking prayers and he could lead you to the
Throne of Grace with quite as sure a step as he had led you
to the heights of merriment.

His wife was a charming, gracious little lady in whose
presence it was impossible to speak an unkind word, even
to think an unkind thought—impossible, in fact, to be less
than your best. Brother Willie worshipped her and very,
very tender was their love for one another. They never
ceased sweethearting, and when an old couple are still
courting after they have passed their golden wedding you
cannot meet them without finding yourself in the presence
of God.

When she died we all wondered what on earth would
happen to Brother Willie. Would his fun fade out? Would
his smile be lost to us? Would his joyous sense of the
ridiculous be gone for good and all?

Nothing like that happened. 'She would not wish me to

be any different,' he would say; 'and I find there are folk in trouble I can help now that I couldn't help before.'

So he transfigured his sorrow, using it and the deeper understanding it gave him to serve still more those brave souls who suffer and do not talk about it. His fun was as merry as ever, though it was but a contact-maker, opening the way to a more wonderful ministry. He became the confidant of many anxious and burdened people, who found it strangely easy to unburden their hearts to him and astonishingly helpful to listen to what he had to say.

An outstanding instance was Brother Willie of a man who was a kindred spirit with his Lord. His was no blind, unintelligent obedience; he knew well enough 'what his Lord doeth' and with a very real sense of partnership furthered the purposes of God with his fun and his exquisite understanding of troubled hearts.

Now he has gone to his reward, bequeathing us all a legacy of smiles. And if there be any shy folk in Heaven who don't feel quite at home (and I don't mind confessing I rather anticipate feeling a bit strange myself at first if I manage to win to it at all), I am sure Brother Willie will be amongst them helping them to settle down. I for one look forward to seeing him in the Father's house. I hope he has not forgotten his lion stories!

CHAPTER XI

DISCIPLINE AND DISCIPLESHIP

'Follow me.'   'Learn of me.'

A NOTHER instance of two very different words spring-ing from the same root. Perhaps in this case the difference is fundamentally one of emphasis, but emphasis is one of the most important things there is. Place it upon discipline and the atmosphere is almost military at once, with a sug-gestion of a sergeant-major barking unintelligible commands; or else it is spartan with the P.T. instructor imposing all sorts of rigorous demands which must be fulfilled. It may have a hundred different settings, but it is always in the realm of penalties and punishments. Think of discipline and that is where the emphasis lies.

Place the accent on discipleship, however, and at once you are thinking of a person, not of a law. A disciple pre-supposes a teacher, a master, a leader. It is true there is again placed before you a mark to be reached, a task to be performed, a lesson to be mastered; it is true that discipline is of the very essence of your loyalty to your chief; but the emphasis is upon the man, your response springs from your respect, your confidence, your affection. You carry out his commands with an enthusiasm the barking sergeant-major can never engender. Most of us are allergic to sergeant-majors.

When I was a very little boy there appeared one day on the dressing-table in my bedroom a neatly printed card entitled 'Manners for Boys'. I read them through: there were ten of them. They all began with 'Don't', but apart from that I remember nothing of them. I recollect trying to conjure up in my imagination the intolerable nit-wit who invented them and succeeded in personifying a gigantic Negative whose pleasure was to stalk through the world to find out what I was doing and tell me to stop it. I took a dim view of his activities and in a few days' time his wretched card mysteriously vanished never to be seen again.

But the gracious lady whom God chose to be my mother, and whose kindly leading in the paths of gentlemanly conduct has meant so much to me all my days, has not faded from my mind like the ten prohibitions. For all I know she probably taught me the same things as the Negative nit-wit sought to do, but the emphasis was different. There was exemplified all the contrast between discipline and discipleship. On the one hand laws and rules and regulations and prohibitions and limitations; on the other a smile and a good-night kiss and 'Cuddle down, bairnies' as you were tucked in at night. Very true is it, as J. M. Barrie has pointed out; that to little boys God has a face very like their mother's.

There is, however, more in it than this. There are few things more moving than to watch the mother's sympathetic handling of the delicate one in the family. It really is one of the fine arts. He cannot stand the rough-and-tumble like the stronger ones and has to be taught very gently what things he cannot do. Yet to carry this too far is to run the risk of making him either embittered and rebellious at his lot or very sorry for himself, neither of which is good. He must not become so obsessed with what he cannot do that he loses sight of what he can do. He must not be so envious of his unhandicapped brothers and sisters that their normal pleasures exasperate him, nor so blind to his own possibilities that he cannot be encouraged to venture. All this needs a sensitiveness of touch of superb quality. Perhaps you have had to be a delicate bairn to realize when you grow up how expert has been the hand that guided you,

and it may be that in this I have the advantage of you. Anyhow, it does make it easier to understand God's dealings
with you if you have had the divine technique exhibited by
your mother.

We have seen, if you have followed our argument thus
far, that if life, for you, can never contain anything better
than second best, yet, nevertheless, God's second best can
still be amazingly good; that if you will make your experience, whatever it is, a starting-point for further experiment, life will be always a thing of increasing surprise and
not the dull, uninteresting thing you feared it might
become; that you may learn what is the will of God for you
so clearly as to leave you in no doubt concerning it and
find it something within your resources; that the foundation
of true greatness is always service; and that your service
need not be an unintelligent observance of rules, but the
keen co-operation of a working-partner and kindred spirit
of Jesus Christ Himself.

In all this there is much to bring reassurance to dismayed
and discouraged folk. But, probably, to look back and see
how winsome has been God's guidance of you—how deft
the touch and how expertly timed which directed your steps
into paths which brought such wondrous ultimate satisfaction—will give you the deepest reassurance of all. For
this cannot become clear without there also dawning upon
you a realization of the amazingly personal interest of God.
It is always an experience both humbling and exhilarating.
'What is man that thou art mindful of him?' cries the
Psalmist, gazing at the night sky with its shining host and
overwhelmed by the immensity of it all. 'Last of all, as unto
one born out of due time, He appeared to me!' exclaims
Paul, almost with a catch in his throat as the thought of the
astonishing condescension of God grips hold of him. 'I felt
my heart strangely warmed,' writes Wesley of his memorable
experience in the meeting-house at Aldersgate Street;

'I felt I did trust in Christ, Christ alone, for salvation; and an assurance was given me that he had taken away *my* sins, even *mine*, and saved *me* from the law of sin and death.'

Luther climbing, upon his knees, Pilate's staircase at Rome to win the Pope's indulgence, leaping to his feet as he realizes 'the just shall live by faith'—the faith that a sinner is pardoned if he will but believe in Christ; Cromwell on his deathbed asking one to read to him from Philippians 'I can do all things through Christ which strengtheneth me'; Abraham Lincoln, broken down as he looked upon the graves of the fallen at Gettysburg and realizing then the great sacrifice of the Son of God; Michael Faraday with his keen scientific mind and his simple, unquestioning assurance of the love of God—these are but taken at random from the great host who have found that life is never the same again when Christ's personal interest in you has passed out of the realm of other men's theories and become one of your own certainties. It is only then that you 'lose the duty in the joy' of your service and the discipline of life He requires of you is lost in the thrill of your discipleship.

This is very surprising when you reflect upon what is involved in Christ's personal interest in us. Let your mind range over the immense variety of people, each with their individual problems, who have found Him adequate to their needs and have been reassured by what they found. For many of them—most of them—face all manner of difficulties which Jesus Himself never had to tackle and have to meet circumstances He never had to encounter. Think of your own perplexities and troubles and you will find most of them never came within His orbit. For instance, we have no difficulty in picturing Him as a comparatively poor man. We need not imagine the little Nazareth home as poverty-stricken, but there appear to have been at least seven children in the family, and no doubt Joseph and Mary had to make the pennies go as far as working-class ingenuity can make them.

But have you ever tried to picture Jesus as a rich man? So far as we know, He never had a rich man's problems to face. Do you think He could have handled them successfully? He had some very pointed things to say about the way riches hindered a man getting into the Kingdom of God. Could He have administered great possessions Himself and yet preserved His spiritual sensitiveness? Most of us have known decent, God-fearing men whom wealth has defeated—would Jesus have been similarly swept away from His moral moorings by inheriting a fortune? He never had that problem to face, but some of you who read this may have had. The personal interest of Christ in us involves that He is interested in the rich man's difficulties as well as in the poor man's—difficulties, that is, He never Himself had to surmount.

We have, of course, on record the advice He once gave to a rich young man whose money was his handicap. 'Give it away!' says Jesus, and it was doubtless the best of counsel in that particular case. But we have no right to argue from the particular to the general and to assume that Christ's recommendation to every wealthy man would be the same. And, anyhow, it is not so easy to give away a fortune without doing more harm than good. The personal interest of Jesus involves that He is acutely alive to how difficult it may be, although He never had it to do.

Again: we all know, for the history of our own times is a terrible commentary upon the fact, how power can corrupt a man. Probably not one man in ten million is fit to be entrusted with it. Jesus, we recall, refused to be placed in the position of a king when the crowd tried their best to press it upon Him. Yet somebody has to administer the government of nations. Imagine Him in the position occupied by any modern king or president. Could He have so handled affairs of State that He could have maintained at one and the same time both the spiritual leadership and

6

the political leadership of His people? He never had it to do—refused to be drawn into it. Yet somebody must face these immense problems. It is impossible to believe in the personal interest of Jesus in us unless we credit Him with a desire to be helpful to burdened men struggling with them.

Again: Jesus died when He was thirty-three, in the full vigour of His physical powers. Have you ever tried to imagine Him as an old man? Could He have faced the problem of old age, with its ever-increasing limitations and subtractions with the same splendid success as He lived out His life as a young man? Could He have found some way of coping with the somewhat chilling necessity of accepting the fact that things you once could take in your stride you now cannot do at all? He never had it to do—many of you have had to.

Yet again: we think of Jesus as a healthy, open-air kind of man who worked hard at a bench, thought nothing of sleeping out of doors, quite instinctively took over the responsibility of the home when Joseph died—a capable, efficient, dependable, and thoroughly adequate person. Can you picture Him as an invalid?

Many of you know how terribly testing that difficult life can be, with all its crippling frustrations and its overwhelming sense of utter futility. Could Jesus have lived out that sort of life without becoming embittered? He never had it to do; some of you have had.

So we might go on—but you can do that for yourself. Imagine Him as a married man with sons away at the front in war-time or needing to be educated and 'placed' in life in peace-time; think of Him as a large employer of labour with all the manifold difficulties attendant upon the handling of great numbers of men; think of Him as a magistrate— 'Who made me a judge over you?' He once asked a man who wanted Him to arbitrate in a family dispute; think of Him as a soldier (if you can, but that is a hard one—still, if He had lived in our country nowadays He would have been called up at eighteen)—in a word, think of Him in any of the settings in which men find themselves and ask: 'Could He have lived my life and made a success of it?' You will find it an interesting field of speculation.

Now here is the surprising thing: His interest in us is so real and practical a thing that, although He never had these problems to face, we all know people who *have* had them to face and who have tackled them successfully in the strength they gained from Him.

Rich men have learnt how to administer their immense and complicated affairs from the poor Carpenter who never had any to manage; the kings and parliaments of the earth have never devised such successful policies as when they have been based upon the principles of Him whose Kingdom is not of this world; old folk have learned from this youth of thirty-three how to grow old gracefully, believing 'the best is yet to be'; the sick and ailing have found in this vigorous son of the open-air a nameless strength; anxious parents have poured out their worries to this young man and have found in Him the answer to their cares; capital and labour have both solved their difficulties with Him at the head of the conference table; judges of men have never reached such sound verdicts as under His guidance; many a great soldier has found Him a reinforcement beyond all other, and some of the greatest names in the last war would set their seal to that.

What does it all mean? How is it that this strange Jesus is found so completely sufficient for all sorts of situations we have to meet which He Himself never encountered? There is no adequate answer—we just know, we who have tried Him, that it is so. The discipline of life is lost in the wonder of discipleship and we begin to understand how right Paul was when he spoke of our being 'more than conquerors through Him that loved us'.

Part Four

Equipment

CHAPTER XII

THE THOUGHT YOU HAVE OF GOD

*'I am no more worthy to be called thy son: make
me as one of thy hired servants.' . . .
. . . 'These many years do I serve thee . . . Yet
thou never gavest me a kid, that I might make merry
with my friends.'*

WE have said that most of our equipment springs from
our handicaps rightly understood. We must now make
good this statement. We have already seen that sometimes
the handicap itself is actually part of our equipment. At
other times it is the means of providing it. But just as an
apprentice must learn what each tool in his craftsman's kit
is for, so you and I, as apprentice Christians, must learn
first of all what is in the tool-box and then what is the
proper use of each tool.

They say you never value your health until you have lost
it. It is not true, but there is truth in it, for it is certainly
the case that the gifts which come uninterruptedly to us
we tend to take for granted with never a thought of grati-
tude. It is not that we are really ungrateful, but we just
forget. If it happens that something disturbs the flow it
dawns upon us at once how regular have been our blessings,
and thus, perhaps, we begin to think.

It is the same with the many courtesies we receive from
those who care for us. We are forgetful of a host of services
which make for our comfort. We accept them as if we had
a right to them and without acknowledgement. Then somebody goes off to a nursing home, or some such happening,

and at once everything begins to go wrong—the gears do not engage, things are not where they ought to be when they ought to be. Again, it dawns upon us what a lot has been done for us.

Not until we are handicapped do we realize how well off we have been. Happy are we if as the result of our awakening we can sing:

> *Ten thousand thousand precious gifts*
> *My daily thanks employ;*
> *Nor is the least a thankful heart,*
> *That takes those gifts with joy.*

For the gift of a thankful heart is an item in the equipment of a Christian which often springs directly from our handicaps. It would be a valuable asset if it merely led to an improvement in our courtesies—but it does far more than that. It forms the habit of relating the gift to the giver, with the obvious result that the giver is never long out of mind. And whereas, in our dealings with our fellows, this, as I say, brightens up our courtesies, when we come to our dealings with our God it results ultimately in a background to life which is completely God-filled. It could not well be otherwise, for, no matter how much we do for one another there can be no comparison with what our Heavenly Father does for us. To form the habit of voicing your thanks to those who serve you—gradually extending it to include café waitresses and bus conductors and the like—will keep you fairly busy; but to thank God for all His gifts would leave you with time for little else!

I once heard, when quite a lad, a dear old parson preach from the text 'Give us this day our daily bread'. It was, he said, a prayer which a rich man ought to pray even more than a poor man. The poor man lives so near the margin that he cannot long forget the Giver whose faithfulness alone saves him constantly from starvation. The rich man, on the other hand, presses buttons and the butler appears; gives his instructions and the meal appears; orders this and that and it is done—and God seems very far away, remote and unnecessary. It is of far more importance to the rich man to remember that there stands One behind all his butlers and servants than it is for the poor man who hasn't any butlers and servants at all, simply because the rich man is so much more likely to forget. He has great need of the gift of a thankful heart to save him from the folly of self-sufficiency.

None of us can afford to let God fade out of our consciousness through the very consistency of His goodness to us. If God were fickle and changeable—or even a bit forgetful now and then—we would have Him much more constantly in mind, because we would be always wondering what He was going to do next—or fail to do next. His faithfulness ought to be our greatest source of thankfulness; it is more often our greatest source of indifference.

I place, therefore, high among the characteristics of a Christian this gift of the thankful heart, constantly alive to the identity of the Giver while in the act of receiving the gift. For it springs from his conception of God and there can be no doubt that the idea of the character of God that you hold will influence you probably more than anything else. It has been well said that the thought you have of God makes you.

To see how this works out, let us turn to the most famous story in the world. If one were asked to name the best-known character in fiction I should think the palm would probably go to the Prodigal Son. He is far more widely known than Shylock or Mr. Pickwick or Sam Weller or Becky Sharp or Jean Valjean or Adam Bede or Sherlock Holmes or any other of the great galaxy of figures who move across the pages of literature. The most curious thing about him, however, is that we have tacked on to him the wrong adjective. He was profligate, not prodigal. Prodigal means merely lavish, wasteful, extravagant, with out the idea of wickedness thrown in. So that, when you come to think of it, the father in the story was more prodigal than the son—which gives us somewhat of a shock when we realize that the father is Christ's own picture of God.

A wasteful, extravagant God! There is no escaping the fact. The details of the portrait are all there. 'He divided unto them his living'—his living, mark you: it seems to any Western businessman an extraordinary thing to do. 'Bring forth the best robe and put it on to him!' he cries in exultation when the wastrel son returns: ring—shoes— fatted calf—was ever such a to do! There was no need for all this extravagance, but, as Jesus paints him in the story, it all comes quite naturally to the father: it is his instinctive reaction—he is just being himself. And even to the elder brother, soured and embittered at the way the family name has been dragged in the mire and not at all inclined to join in the festivities, there is the same open-handed uncalcu- lating attitude: 'All that I have is thine.'

If anyone but Christ had drawn such a portrait of God we should have ridiculed it. And even He took a risk when He drew it for us, for it is only our better selves that are fit to be entrusted with it. There have always been those who have seized upon it as something which provided a con- venient elasticity in the moral law. Forgiveness is God's job and the sinner is merely giving Him the opportunity to function. It is all very cheap and hollow and shabby, and, anyhow, Paul riddled it with his devastating phrase about 'sinning that grace may abound'. Moreover, it is a stupid notion really, for a moment's thought will remind us that God is always out for our own good and it is certainly not good for us that we shall escape the consequences of our own foolery so completely as to give us the impression that it didn't matter. One of the best sermons I ever heard on the Prodigal Son was from the text 'Be not deceived, God is not mocked'. There was more challenging discernment in the mere choice of the text than there is in many discourses I have heard—and in many I have delivered, for that matter.

We are wise if we keep very much in mind when we are thinking of the prodigality of God—His open-handed, lavish generosity—the solemn fact that He is *not* mocked by His own moral law. It is when we have fooled about with our health, prostituted our faculties, soiled our minds, loved the wrong things, and laughed at life's sanctities that we come to ourselves with a shock and find ourselves wanting the wholesome things we once knew, but now living in a land where there is a famine of them. It is then that our sense of stewardship, outraged and neglected, sweeps back over us like a great wave and we realize what a poverty-stricken affair we have made of life. At long last we are in the mood to listen to our better self—and therefore are fit to be entrusted with Christ's portrait of God. For now we are not inclined to make demands upon God—'Give me the portion that falls to me'—but rather to invite God to make demands upon us for a change: 'No more worthy to be called thy son, make me as one of thy hired servants.' So, after all, God is not mocked. The risk Jesus took in the painting of the portrait of the Prodigal Father justifies itself. Our unworthy self sought to exploit it: our best self is inspired to service by it. The very reception we receive at His hands, the complete and unhesitating forgiveness He gives us, shame us all the more.

The same joyous pardon, however, only irritates and exacerbates the elder brother. And again we see, by the very contrast between these two lads, how true it is that the thought you have of God makes you. For this son, with all his fine qualities, completely fails to rise to the heights of great nobility, and the real reason is that he had a wrong estimate of his father. The younger son came home asking to be made a servant: the elder stayed at home never regarding himself as anything else. 'Lo, these many years do I serve thee,' he growls, sullen and rebellious. It is quite clear what he thought of his father—the old man was an exacting task-master, making constant demands and granting few rewards. You only need to think of God that way and your whole life will be robbed of its enchantment.

'All that I have is thine,' the father reminds him: for he had divided to them his living. But for once the father was inaccurate. One thing he had which the elder lad had not inherited—his father's spirit. It is the greatest tragedy in the whole story. Not the wastrel's despair nor the father's broken heart can equal in poignancy the elder son's refusal to come into the sunshine of reunion.

He sees his father, hard and severe on him, soft and over-lenient with his brother. He was wrong on both counts. But the thought you have of God makes you.

It is the first foundation quality in the equipment of a Christian: his conception of the character of God. It colours everything else in life. And that is why a thankful heart which forms the habit of constantly relating the gifts to the giver is itself one of God's greatest gifts.

CHAPTER XIII

A MIND CONTENT

'I know how to be abased, and I know also how to abound.'

IT may surprise some of us to be told that one of the chief elements in the equipment of a Christian is a contented mind. Immediately some of us will be up in arms against such a suggestion. A contented mind is a handicap. It is the enemy of all ambition, all progress, all enterprise, all initiative. It is the old notion of religion being the opiate of the people—mere dope. The old, out-worn idea, which never was true, of

> *The rich man in his castle,*
> *The poor man at his gate,*
> *God made them, high or lowly,*
> *And order'd their estate.*

No doubt God has ordained that some men should be rich and has given them the faculty to administer great estates. But, equally doubtless, some men have great possessions which they ought never to have, for they have no idea how to handle them and their antics give some point to the cynicism that you can tell what God thinks of money when you look at the people He has given it to. That remark is, of course, manifestly unfair, but it is no concern of a cynic to be fair: he counts himself smart only when he makes other people smart. Nevertheless, the notion seems fairly deep-seated in the minds of most of us that a contented mind would go much more easily with wealth than with poverty. It is not so; but most folk would like the opportunity of trying it out at first hand.

But this question of a contented mind goes deeper than that. Have we any right to be content in a world gone so far wrong as this? Does it not imply a spineless acceptance of conditions which ought rather to make each of us a most militant rebel? Was not Jesus Himself one of the most discontented men who ever lived? Discontent of a noble sort was His, for it arose, by the most glorious paradox, from a mind more content than has ever been known before or since. 'My meat,' said He, 'is to do the will of Him that sent me'; 'My Father worketh hitherto and I work'; 'I and the Father are one'; 'Believe me that I am in the Father and the Father in me—or else believe me for the very works' sake.' No one could speak like that who was not completely content. Yet: 'Ye have heard that it was said of old time, but *I* say unto you'; 'O Jerusalem, how often would I have gathered thy children together—but ye would not'; 'O that thou hadst known in this day even thou the things which belong unto peace.' What a fierce discontent is here!

Quite obviously a contented mind springs from no spiritless resignation to anything that may just happen along. To regard as divinely ordained everything, no matter how unjust or calamitous, which comes your way, and to bow meekly to it because you feel it must be God's will is to make nonsense both of the moral law and the character of God. It is to make the highest virtue a sort of jellyfish inertia—hardly as good as that, indeed, for even a jellyfish can sting. Frustration of the good is never the divine will— therefore acceptance of it can be no part of our business. We have no right to acquiesce in a failure which insults the God in whose image we are made.

We turn with a certain interest, therefore, to the words of a very great craftsman in the art of Christian living— whose life, incidentally, was a far stormier journey than most of us will ever have to tread. 'I have learned,' said he, 'in whatsoever state I am, therein to be content. I know how to be abased and I know also how to abound.' This is no 'prentice hand at the craft of discipleship. This man has mastered the art. 'I know how,' he says, and therein lies the rub.

If frustration makes you discouraged and disheartened, it is because you do not know *how* to be frustrated. If deprivation makes you embittered, it is because you do not know *how* to be deprived. If to be passed over leaves you feeling sore and slighted, it is because you do not know *how* to be passed over. If to be ordinary makes you jealous, it is because you do not know *how* to be ordinary. In all these things and hundreds like them there is an art, something to be learned. You have to know how if you are to receive them with a contented mind.

And similarly, if always getting your own way makes you arrogant and intolerant it is because you do not know how to direct. If abundance of this world's goods makes you conceited and self-important, it is because you do not know how to possess. If to be honoured and exalted makes you pompous and proud, it is because you do not know how to receive honours. In these things too, and hundreds like them, there is an art, something to be learned. Again you have to know how if you are to receive them with a contented mind.

This Paul of Tarsus claimed that he did know how. His secret is worth knowing if we can find it out. It is, in fact, one of the major items of our equipment. It lies, actually, within the very word 'content'. With the accent on the last syllable it means 'satisfied'; on the first it means 'holding capacity' or, in the plural, 'things held' as we speak of the 'contents' of a book. In the mind of Paul both ideas blend. He is satisfied if he feels himself 'held'. So long as he is sure of the Everlasting Arms around him and beneath him he is completely indifferent to everything else. He is content because of these Everlasting Arms he is the content. If God holds him in position, that is all he wants: what that position is, is God's affair, not Paul's.

Well, but you say, you are not making out your case at all. Are you not back again to the old position of 'rich man at his castle, poor man at his gate'? You have come round full circle to the opiate of the people idea—putting up with any mortal thing which happens to you in the belief that it is God's will and that it must therefore be for the best. This species of contentment is nothing else than resignation to anything that may just happen along—the very attitude you have just described as making nonsense of the moral law and the character of God.

It is really poles apart from any such thing. For just as Jesus felt His one-ness with the Father to be the source of His own content of mind, yet found that very contentment to be, in turn, the source of His fierce discontent with all that frustrated God's will, so Paul felt with regard to Jesus. 'Christ liveth in me,' he cried, with Christ's own sense of a God-filled life repeated, so to speak, a stage farther down the scale. There is the basis of his contented mind. But you can no more accuse Paul of a spineless acceptance of things which cry aloud for resistance than you could have accused Jesus of it. He was a 'bonny fechter', was Paul. To put it in a nutshell, he was certainly content—but he was content to be a rebel, just as his Lord had been before him.

He who can detect no difference in this attitude from what we have described as jellyfish inertia is surely somewhat slow in the uptake. For see how it works out. 'I know how to be abased,' he says—and he means far more than that he has been poor and ignored and thwarted and insulted and has learnt how to put up with it. As we have just seen, the common result of such experience is to make us disheartened, embittered, sore, and jealous. Nothing like that came to Paul. They fling him into prison and he sings in it—and before long he is leading the jailer to Christ. He does not accept the prison with patient dumb resignation: he expects to find in it some work to do for God. He is shipwrecked in a storm which they would have avoided if the captain of the vessel had had the wits he was born with; but he is not embittered at his life being endangered by another's folly. He, a landsman, calmly takes charge of a critical situation and by his faith in God steadies the whole crew and avoids a panic. We have already seen what he made of the soldiers chained to him in his long imprisonment awaiting trial and how, instead of becoming merely discouraged and depressed by frustration, he gets the Gospel wormed into the very household of Nero. All along the initiative remains with him. He is no cork upon the wave, flung here and flung there: he is no puppet who must dance when others pull the strings. He knows how to be abased because in the very circumstance of his humiliation he finds avenues of service. You cannot defeat a man like that. Lower his circumstances as you will, he knows how to live in them, and to live usefully at that. There is all the difference in the world between regarding the things which come your way as something to be endured and seeing them as something to be used.

Similarly, he knows how to abound. This is difficult to learn. Read again *Little Dorrit* if you would see how difficult it is: see how the prisoner of the Marshalsea, come at length to fortune, cuts so pompous a figure and lords it over everybody merely because he now owns more than they. The old Lancashire saying, 'Clogs to clogs in three generations', pithily points the same truth. The first generation, in clogs, works hard and makes money; the second, with grand ideas and little gumption—more wishbone than backbone, as they say—wastes it; the third is back to clogs again because the second did not know 'how

to abound'. But there is more to it than this. Many a man
who does not lose his head through his abundance would
nevertheless, in Paul's judgement, still be classed as one
who 'does not know how'. The test is the same as in knowing
how to be abased—do you find, in the very circumstance
of your abundance, avenues of service to God and your
fellows? Does the initiative remain with you? Or are you
more inclined, when you find yourself well off, to demand
more service and to give less? Was it not John Stuart Mill
who spoke of those who 'equate privilege with merit
rather than with responsibility'? It is the great temptation
of those who have great possessions: to persuade yourself
that you really deserve all this good fortune, and so never
come within miles of 'knowing how to abound'.

But if you feel yourself 'held' in a position of great
administrative importance, held there by God Himself,
you cannot long waste your time by Jack-Hornerish self-
congratulation—'What a good boy am I!'—for it is a
significant fact that God never rewards faithful discipleship
with £ s. d. 'The only money of God is God,' said Emerson
in his striking way; 'and He never pays with anything else.'
You may by your Christian integrity and your native ability
combined win through to great business success; but it is
not God who sends you business success—what He sends
you is more and more of His spirit, and if the conduct of
your affairs as directed by Him wins for you the business
confidence of your fellows and growing success follows,
well and good. To the Christian, however, business promi-
nence is not an end in itself. It brings influence and responsibility, and the more of that you acquire the more of the
Spirit of God you need to cope with it. That is why it is so
hard for a rich man to enter the Kingdom of Heaven—he so
seldom manages to keep pace in spiritual power with
material success. But the rich man who sees in his situation
the hand of God, feels in it the holding grasp of God, has

no difficulty in doing it. He knows how to abound; he is content.

A contented mind, therefore, is undisturbed by circumstance because it is sure of God, always conscious of God, ever at work for God. He who possesses it does not live in a world where he just must accept whatever hits him. He is the initiator all the time; he is an implacable rebel against all injustice and evil. He would not have it otherwise. It is part of his equipment. It is the way the Master went—should not the servant tread it still?

CHAPTER XIV

YE SHALL RECEIVE POWER

*'When they beheld the boldness of Peter and John
. . . they took knowledge of them, that they had been
with Jesus.'*

SINCE, as we have seen, a contented mind is one of the
primary elements in the equipment of a Christian, it is
soon abundantly clear that we cannot long remain contented
unless we are accomplishing more than in our old days of
frustration. It is not much use honestly believing that God
has a work for us to do in whatever circumstances we find
ourselves unless at the same time we feel to be furnished
with the power to make something of it. I can imagine no
more humiliating experience than to be promoted to a
bigger position and then to find yourself unable to hold the
job down; nor any more exhilarating experience than
finding yourself able to rise to it and take it in your stride.

Nobody, however, can be very long at the business of
trying to live the Christian life without finding out that
the demands of Jesus are so exacting that only by securing
a moral power additional to our own can we ever hope to
meet them. Our next step is therefore to find out (or to
refresh our memory), to discover or to rediscover what
resources Christianity has to offer and how they can be
laid hold of. Again we find out that it is true that our
equipment springs from our handicap. It is because we realize
we are *powerless* that we realize we must cast about for
sources of power.

If you have ever given the matter a thought you must have

envied the early disciples their first-hand contact with Jesus. We have all met people of such inspiring personality that we felt instinctively we could not be less than our best in their presence. It was said of Forbes Robinson that he gave you the impression of being so interested in you that he compelled you to be interested in yourself. He saw such possibilities in you that you came to believe in them yourself. He took your best so much for granted that you realized that less than your best just wouldn't do. If one man could produce that effect upon another, what must it have been to have lived in the company of Jesus as did His contemporary followers?

Not that it was always easy or fascinating or even uplifting. I think Jesus must have been difficult to live with. If we are honest with ourselves we find He still is, and I do not imagine it was any simpler to be with Him walking the streets and lanes of Palestine in the days of His flesh. It cannot have been very easy to live with one who was always right, so that, if you differed with him at all, you were bound to be wrong. We like to come out on top now and again, but in any conflict with Him that would never happen. And then again, He would never take advice—and we do so love to give it! Yet when poor old Peter, horrified at the prospect of opposition, persecution, and murder which Jesus foresaw for Himself, remonstrated with Him, he is scorched by the fierce rebuke: 'Get you behind me, you hindrance—you think like a man; you don't think as God thinks!' It is not easy to stand that sort of thing when you are simply trying to be helpful. Would-be disciples are given the cold douche of realism when they come full of new-found enthusiasm: amazing bursts of popularity, reaching almost hysterical levels so that He could have been enthroned as a national leader, are just rejected as being the wrong kind of success: He chooses to consort with the riff-raff and people of more than doubtful reputation—in short, He does the most unaccountable and unpredictable things and seems to have no idea of prudence or discretion. No, not at all easy to live with, and a lot of people gave it up as a bad job and 'walked no more with Him'. Yet when he asked the queerly assorted group of twelve men whether they also were going to leave Him, He found the idea of going back was in the mind of not one of them. Easy to live with or not, they found in His presence a something they had come across nowhere else and it gripped them like the pull of a magnet.

For even if they were constantly finding themselves in the wrong they could not fail to realize they were becoming bigger men all the time. Even if they could not so much as guess what He was going to do next, they found they were living in a larger world by being near Him. Even the gibe that they thought like men and not like God set them wondering because, after all, they *were* men and the criticism could have no point had it not been possible for them to think like God—an idea which had not so much as floated across their minds.

Go away! To whom should they go? No one else could usher them into so wonderful a world; no one else could teach them such a marvellous way of living; He made them into 'growing' men and no one else could do it.

That was why, when He was murdered, their little world fell so completely to pieces. They had nothing left. In the courtyard of the High Priest's house Peter wriggled and squirmed and twisted and evaded and became confused and embarrassed, cursed and swore under the taunts of a pert serving-maid, and when the company round the fire saw the shamefaced cowardice of Peter they took knowledge of him that he had been with Jesus. But Jesus was on His way to the Cross and Peter had lost everything.

And that was why, when He had come back, and with Him all the uprush of new hope and new confidence and new vision and new purpose and new horizons—that was why they found their shattered world restored again so that 'in Him all things held together', as Paul later put it. They were growing men again and when men beheld the boldness of Peter they took knowledge of him that he had been with Jesus. Take Jesus from them: they are left with confusion of face, completely broken men—as must inevitably be the lot of him who has followed Christ and lost touch with Him. Bring back Jesus and their whole bearing is altered—heads erect, steady of eye, absolutely fearless men. Nobody but Jesus could do that for them.

Nobody but He can do it for *you*. But the very last thing He said on earth was just this reassurance we most need: 'Ye shall receive power when the Holy Ghost is come upon you.'

It is the very thing we want: the promise of reinforcement so that we can rise to the exacting demands which face us. The amazing experience of Christ's contemporary disciples who knew Him at first-hand may be ours too in these modern days. Nor is this merely a preacher's way of putting things—a mere figure of speech, poetic licence, what you will—anything but what it says. The wonder of the Gospel is that it *does* mean what it says—namely, that Jesus is alive: that you can have His companionship and His reinforcement of your powers just as they had.

In those wonderful days after the Resurrection when He was constantly coming and going, breaking in upon them without warning and in the most surprising fashion, they must have lived in a positive fever of expectancy. They would engage in no task they would not have liked to be found busy with if He appeared; they would start no conversation they would not have liked Him to share in should they suddenly find Him with them: they would go to no place they would not like Him to have discovered them in. So they gradually found themselves, during that time when they did not know whether, next minute, He would be there or not, living as though He were there all the time. And, naturally enough, there could have been no better method of coming to realize that He *was* there all the time—so that when He finally went away from them and the well-loved form was seen no more, they had none of the feeling of sickening loneliness which floods over us as we turn away sometimes when a train has steamed out and we realize we shall never see that waving figure again. We all know what it is to go numbly back to our work feeling the world has become suddenly empty. They had known it when the horror of the Crucifixion came home to them: they had no such feelings at the Ascension. They had learnt that His visible presence was not necessary—His actual presence was just as real without it. It had, in fact, become even more so. Previously He had been with them or not with them as the case might be; now He was in them and you could no more get Him out than you could, in B. G. Sandhurst's startling phrase, 'get the rattiness out of a rat'. Small wonder they had no sense of separation.

Others found the secret too. 'Nothing shall separate us!' cried Paul. 'Christ living in *me*!' is his amazing discovery (we keep coming back to it) and obviously if that be any more than a figure of speech—another preacher's way of putting things—it does solve the whole problem of meeting the exacting demands of Jesus which we have found too much for us. If it be true that Christ can take possession of your personality just as a tenant takes possession of a house —*lives in it* as Paul says—you will, without difficulty, think as God thinks, for you will have the mind that was in Christ actually functioning in your own brain: it could not be otherwise. And if that should happen to you, the demands of Jesus cannot possibly continue to be far beyond your capacity because the One who makes these demands is now the One in control of your life and therefore it is up to Him to carry them out. And that is how you receive power when the Holy Ghost is come upon you.

But, I think I hear you say, 'That would be indeed good news if it were true—but nothing like that ever happened to me'. Well, perhaps not. But why not? It has happened to thousands of folk just as ordinary as you and me: folk of no special mystic qualities, no hyper-sensitive spirituality. Moreover, they are not all in the past tense. I know many people to whom it has happened; and if you don't, it is probably because you have looked for them in the wrong place, or haven't looked at all. Why should it not happen to you? Be honest with yourself—do you *want* it to happen? Christ never burgles a man's personality; you must invite Him in and He was always One to insist that you realize what you are doing before you bid Him enter. The poet Lysaght says

> *Pause ere you draw the bolt and bid him rest,*
> *If in your old content you would remain*

speaking about welcoming love into your life and, when you think of it, there is not much difference between welcoming love or welcoming Christ. 'Not alone he enters.'

'Do you *want* to be healed?' Christ asked a man who had lain thirty-eight years at the pool. Not such a foolish question as it sounds; indeed, a very searching question. Thirty-eight years is a long time. A man can get used to being a passenger through life in much less time than that. To receive power—to become a fit man—means the end of all that: the end of being carried by other people. If you are fit you will have to work, to shoulder responsibility, to pull your weight, to live in a bigger world—to face more exacting demands than you ever faced before. Think it out. Do you really want it to happen to you? You are taking something on if it does. Was it not Huxley who said: 'It does not take much of a man to be a Christian, but it takes all there is of him.' Are you prepared for the upheaval in your life which your acceptance of Christ's offer of spiritual power involves?

But I must not forget that this is a book for discouraged people, who if they have bothered to read this far are, I hope, feeling reassured and ready for fresh adventures, with hearts that are brave again. For people, in short, who do not need to be told to think it out, for you have already done so and have decided to go ahead. Well, the promise is for you: ye shall receive power. I have seen it happen many a time.

I knew a man who lost a lad in the First World War. On the anniversary of his death he lost another. About the same time his daughter's health broke down and under the strain his wife collapsed. His world was pretty well in ruins, but his foundations stood. Another friend, who himself knew something about the forty-second Psalm, sought him out and put into his hands a little volume by that choice soul Percy Ainsworth, from which in his own dark hour he had drawn strength. The stricken man read it through at a sitting and at once realized that here was comfort and reinforcement of soul—power to see it through. So he had some little cards printed of extracts which had steadied him and reassured him, and these he gave away as he met, from time to time in his business contacts—'folk whose burden is heavier than mine'. 'You would be surprised,' said this Greatheart, 'how many I meet.'

Such equipment as this can only come from a handicap accepted and rightly understood. Such a man was, in all his overwhelming sorrows, the possessor of a contented mind, for he was sure of his God: he retained the initiative and found himself equipped with power to use it. Triumphant living is that.

CHAPTER XV

THE THREE GUIDES

'I am with you always'

THE Christian who has a right idea of the character of God, who has reached the state of mind when he is content to be where he is because he realizes that, whatever his circumstances, God has a work for him to do in that situation; and who has become conscious of an inflow of power into his life enabling him to cope with every opportunity which presents itself, is indeed to be congratulated on his prospects. No matter what his handicap, he finds himself living in a fascinating world. Life, which in his early days of dismay at the limitations which faced him, had seemed to have gone so suddenly empty, has become rich again. It is filled with a consciousness of God which was never his before. For he finds added to his newly found riches a new sense of certainty taking the place of that divided mind which so bothered him before.

It is the merest platitude to say that very few of life's decisions are between good and bad. Not often are the issues so clear-cut as that. It is generally between good and better: sometimes, even, between bad and worse. We come to life's cross-roads, but they do not cross at right angles, when our own common sense and native sense of direction would be probably enough to keep us right. Rather do we often find them facing us at an acute angle, and at the point where we have to choose, it is not easy to decide which leads in the right direction—they both appear to do; and which one will, sooner or later, turn aside and take us far astray. So that a sense of certainty about which way to take is obviously an item of equipment of immense value. Like the rest we have noted, it arises out of our very handicap, for it is our original perplexity at our position that first sets us casting round for guidance. As we have already seen, we feel instinctively that it would be unworthy of God to leave us floundering about in hopeless bewilderment when we are really anxious to know what is the Christian thing to do. We feel it to be eminently reasonable for us to ask: 'If a man wants to do what is right, can he be *sure*?'

God, however, speaks to us in a variety of ways. He sends us guides of different types, but they all have the authentic note. It is our business so to attune our ear that we can recognize it. This chapter is an attempt to be helpful along that line.

I once heard a beautiful allegory from the late A. E. Whitham. He told of a traveller called upon to journey into a far country. And because he had to travel alone and because he had no map, and because he had heard there were no signposts in that land, he went to consult the Oracle that he might find reassurance that he had not missed his way.

'Truly, my son,' replied the Oracle, 'you have no need to fear. As you journey, keep your eyes fixed upon a certain star—travel always towards the star—and you shall walk in safety and shall not miss your way.'

'But,' objected the traveller; 'what if I must travel through the storm and the storm wrack blot out the star—what then?'

'If it should be,' said the Oracle, 'that such be your lot and the storm wrack cover the heavens and blot out the star, still are you not without your guide. For here and there and yonder, down the valley that you must travel, are the cottages of the peasant folk. And at nightfall they place in the windows the cottage lamps. If, therefore, my son, you must travel through the storm and the storm wrack shall blot our your star—you can find your way by the cottage lamps, and shall walk in safety and shall not miss your road.'

'But,' said the traveller, 'suppose I must travel through the storm and the star be blotted out—and suppose the cottage folk have forgotten the lamps—what then?'

'Even then,' replied the Oracle, 'you are not without your guide. For down the valley that you must travel blows a prevailing wind. Keep the wind from the heath upon your cheek and your direction will be sure, even though the star be blotted out and the peasant folk have forgotten the lamps. Journey in safety, my son. You shall not miss your way.'

Three guides: the star in the heaven, the cottage lamps, and the wind on the heath. Let them serve as types, for they are as varied as needs be to illustrate God's widely different approaches to us. The star—distant, remote, aloof, uninfluenced by anything we can do or say or think—no more affected by the passions of men or the agonies of men than by our brandishing our puny swords at it or cursing its indifference to our sufferings. The cottage lamp—homely, intimate, on our own level, provided by our fellow men, familiar, friendly, understandable. The breath upon your cheek, of the wind from the heath—something acutely personal to yourself: not seen by you, but *felt* by you; not dependent on others, but sensed by your own consciousness. In such varied, widely different ways does God direct us, and if our spirit be but sensitive enough we may journey with perfect confidence though the way be strange and we travel through a country we know not.

We have need at times of a guide that we cannot influence, cannot alter, cannot affect—cannot, in fact, do anything with except just accept. Like the star to the traveller, it is there and nothing can make it not there. You may rail at it, storm at it, scoff at it, ignore it, ridicule it—you are met with silence. You may argue about it—pretend it isn't there at all—turn your back upon it: still silence and it is still there. Storms may obscure it for a time, but they pass and it endures. We have need, I say, of such a guide as this. And one is there to reassure us—a great historic fact: the fact of Christ. It is there and nothing can make it not there. Men have railed at it, stormed, scoffed, sneered at it, ignored it, ridiculed it, argued about it, pretended it wasn't there at all; the smoke and dust of war has obscured it, but nations have sunk back exhausted and the reek of battle has blown away; and men, again learning to look upwards, have found the fact still there, uninfluenced by all the clamour and insane din. We can still step in to a travel agency and book a ticket to the places that He knew; we can still tread the roads He trod, climb the hillsides where He spent so many lonely hours, walk the grim way He marched, surrounded by the spears of Roman soldiers, as He carried His own gibbet to the Hill of the Skull. This is history and there is nothing you can do about it—but accept it. But there come to most folk at one time or another periods of spiritual staleness and flatness when a kind of miasma of unreality seems to settle down upon everything and it is easy to drift into uncertainty even about the great foundation truths of the Christian faith. Then it is good to remind oneself of simple things, plain, honest-to-goodness hard historic facts. You don't question the historic fact of Napoleon nor his defeat at Waterloo—it is no better established than the fact of Christ. You don't scruple to accept as historic the assassination of Lincoln—it is no better documented than the Crucifixion of Jesus. If you are wondering whether you are standing on shifting sand, get back to simple facts and build up again from them. You cannot make a fact into a not-fact. Christianity is built on facts. Like the star in the heavens they can be to you a guide along your journey.

'But what if I must travel through the storm and the storm wrack blots out the star—what then?'

The star is a very impressive guide—but it is a very cold and impassive thing: very constant, but a long way off: quite uninfluenced by the rise and fall of Empires, but very impersonal—unhelpful if you want companionship. The witness of History is impressive but it, too, is cold and remote: it may convince your reason but it does not warm your heart. And if it be that you must travel through the storm you are apt to lose sight of it. Not many people in times of trouble and sorrow are drawn to study the evidences of Christianity. What then?

'Here and there and yonder, down the valley that you must travel are the cottages of the peasant folk. And at nightfall they place in the windows the cottage lamps. . . . You can find your way by them and shall walk in safety and shall not miss your road.'

Here is guidance of a very different order. This is not remote and aloof but familiar and friendly and on our own level. There is nothing here of cold, impressive grandeur: this is a warm, human contact; you are dependent for it upon flesh-and-blood people like yourself; it may even fail you if the cottage folk are thoughtless, but you are prepared to risk all that because it is something that you can so easily understand. It makes you feel at home and gives you a delightful sense of companionship.

It may be for this very reason that we so often fail to see God's hand in it when His guidance reaches us through human channels—until, perhaps, we sit down and think things out and it begins to dawn upon us that something rather queer has happened.

I heard once of a man who was very happily married. He and his wife were ideally suited and their delight in each other was very beautiful to see. Quite suddenly she died and his little world just fell to pieces. His faith fell to pieces too, and the depth of his previous joy was the measure of the bitterness of soul that now swept over him. A great rebellion against a God who could trample down such exquisite happiness surged up within him. For days he wandered about the streets of the city consumed with grief and rage and impotent revolt. He had believed in a God of love—he had been deceived by a Brute who jeered at his agony; he had believed in a God of purpose—he now found a devilish frustration of all purpose; he had thought God was just—he had learnt He was ruthless, vindictive, inhuman.

In this savage mood he walked sullen and morose down a city street when he saw a man whom he scarcely knew dart out of the stream of traffic and come towards him. Never had he done more than pass the time of day with this man, a mere nodding acquaintance. But he came up, obviously to offer his sympathy. He tried to speak, but his words choked in his throat—the other's misery was too much for him and he could not say a word. All he could do was to seize the hand of the bereaved man, then hurry away, quite overcome.

The stricken man stood gazing after him till he was lost in the crowd: then looked at his own hand still tingling with the grasp of sympathetic understanding. Slowly the significance of the simple little incident began to dawn upon him.

'Why did that fellow do that? I scarcely know the man; he is nothing to me; I've never said more than "Good-day" to him in my life. Yet my trouble takes such a hold on him that he tries to help me and cannot say a word. What's it got to do with him, anyhow? My loss isn't his loss. No need for him to be cut up about it. But he *is* cut up about it. His handshake spoke volumes. . . .' And there sprang into his mind an odd phrase from Browning: 'What if that hand be—God!'

Ay, what if it be? Perhaps God was cut up about it too. Perhaps He was not the heartless, brutal monster he had imagined—perhaps God Himself had purposes which were broken off by the death that had shattered his own. Was God as broken-hearted as himself? Was God trying to say something to him which he had not yet imagined? Had God sent to him this chance acquaintance who tried to speak and could not—whose only message was through the grip of his hand? What if that hand be God?

In some such way comes to us the word of God, the reassurance of God, the guidance of God through the ministry of our fellow men. It is the guidance of the cottage lamps—warm, friendly, homely, intimate, capable of failing altogether if the other fellow is not alive to the opportunity or not sensitive enough to discern it, or even too shy to venture. Yet how real can God become when His messenger knows his job and has the artist touch.

Most of us have had friends of this order. Truly did Kipling sing:

> *One man in a thousand, Solomon says,*
> *Will stick more close than a brother.*
> *And it's worth while seeking him half your days*
> *If you find him before the other.*

If you have ever known a man or woman who lived a better life than you were doing—the kind of person who cannot come into the room without lifting the moral tone of it, and yet manages to do so without parade of piety— then take note of them: they have lit a cottage lamp for you and you may travel by its light.

'But suppose I must travel through storms and the star be blotted out—and suppose the cottage folk have forgotten the lamps. What then?'

It may be that this little book may perchance fall into the hands of one who has had no such friend: no saintly mother to surround him with her prayers, no strong friend to steady him in the rough days; just nobody.

I heard of a man once, during the First World War, who was in the same battalion as a friend of mine. He did not seem to have a relative or friend in the world. He never got a letter, and when in the front line the mail arrived and the welcome messages from home were given over to eager hands, he would shrink away ashamed that nobody thought him worth writing to. My friend told me of this and I decided to surprise the lad, so I wrote to him though we were complete strangers. I did not think it would do him any harm to realize that somebody thought it worth while. It was not, I dare say, a very remarkable letter, merely a 'curtain raiser', so to speak, designed to make a contact and possibly lead on to something more. It never, however, led to anything at all. He was killed the day before it arrived.

I mention him because there are folks like that who just seem to be left out of friendship's circle. It is a queer thing, but there they are and something has to be done about them. God must do something anyway, even if we don't. No star —no cottage lamp—what then?

'Even then you are not without your guide. For down the valley that you must travel blows a prevailing wind. Keep the wind from the heath upon your cheek and your direction will be sure, even though the star be blotted out and the peasant folk have forgotten the lamps. Journey in safety, my son. You shall not miss your way.'

Here is guidance of yet another order: no distant, unalterable historic fact like a star in the heavens; no simple friendly but fallible help like the lamp in the window. Here is something acutely personal, something you may feel within your very being as you feel the breath upon your cheek, something for you alone. The witness of history may leave you completely unimpressed; you may never have had a friend who made God real to you; but there is within you, wrought into the very stuff of your being, an instinct for goodness. Call it what you will—fairplay, decency, old-school-tie, team-spirit, whatever you like— there it is and you must account for it somehow. If you have ever taken an action or refrained from taking an action (whichever way it was) so that someone else might benefit, you have followed the guidance of an impulse as completely personal to you as the feeling of the wind from the heath upon your cheek. No fact of history prompted it, no friend suggested it. You *felt* it to be right and you followed what you felt.

Perhaps you would be surprised to be told the Holy Spirit had anything to do with it. Yet it is still true that

> *Every virtue we possess,*
> *And every conquest won,*
> *And every thought of holiness,*
> *Are His alone.*

You are oftener in the hands of God than you think you are. That is why it is of such importance to learn to detect His presence, to recognize His touch, to attune your ear to His voice. Do that and you will travel safely.

CHAPTER XVI

DO YOU REALIZE HOW RICH YOU ARE?

' All things are yours '

THE scope of the Christian's equipment is now, I hope, becoming clear. But there rises the uneasy question which stands at the head of this chapter, and before we go any farther it would be as well to face it with all that it implies. As a matter of fact, it implies a good deal, and the bother Paul had with the Church at Corinth is an illustration apt enough for our purpose.

There is a curious twist in our nature which makes us lay hold of so little when we are heirs to so much. We would count a man the stupidest of fellows who, possessed of the completest set of craftsman's tools, nevertheless chose to select only a few to work with and so to limit his effectiveness in quite unnecessary fashion. Yet this was what they did at Corinth when they split their Church up into cliques. They fell to squabbling among themselves as to the relative merits of some of their ministers, and partisanship got so hot that it bade fair to destroy the family spirit of the Church—as cliques in a Church always do. It was not to be wondered at that the men they had 'sat under' (as Scots folk would say) should arouse individual preferences. Men of widely different types always do that, particularly if each be a notable example of his type. And they had had some very notable men at Corinth: Paul himself to begin with— a great missionary pioneer, a great organizer, a great teacher, a great Church-builder. Perhaps not a great orator: he himself admits he came amongst them not with excellency

113

of speech lest their faith should rest upon the gifts of men rather than upon the gift of God. Whether he could do it but would not or whether he just was not a great orator we do not know. He was a great thinker, but not every great thinker can thrill a crowd. Anyhow they came to think of him as no great spell-binder. And Paul himself admitted further that he 'fed them with milk not with meat', so by the time they could take stronger stuff they may have come to regard his preaching as rather elementary. Particularly as he would be bound to suffer by comparison with Apollos, who followed after: Apollos the silver-tongued, an orator indeed, whose fame still lives. That, of course, was real preaching. He could do it: knew how to get it across, as we say. Then Peter is thought to have been there, though this is not certain. But some opponents of Paul who knew Peter fastened upon the fact that Peter had been a close disciple of Jesus, whereas Paul never had been, and, like a number of folk one meets with, they could think of no way of talking up their own favourite except by discrediting Paul. And then, to crown all, others tried to cut away from this partisan spirit by a return to Jesus Himself and formed a Christ-party, but only succeeded in putting Jesus at the head of yet another clique.

All this tomfoolery distresses Paul, this formation of a Paul-party and an Apollos-party and a Peter-party and a Christ-party. 'After all,' he cries, 'what is Apollos? What is Paul? Ministers through whom ye believed; and each as the Lord gave to him. . . . Let no man glory in men. For all things are yours, whether Paul or Apollos, or Cephas or the world or life or death or things present or things to come; all are yours: and ye are Christ's and Christ is God's.'

A strange business this, to be heirs to so much yet possessors of so little. For, of course, a thing may be yours —given to you, entrusted to you—but until you have appropriated it, used it, made it your own, you have not really possessed it.

Permit a very homely illustration. The morning service was over in the little country chapel and the preacher went to dinner with a bluff old farmer. He was shown into the drawing-room. It was chilly and damp through disuse, the chimney smoked, and the fire sulked at being asked to burn in so unfamiliar a grate. The tables in the room—'occasional tables' they call them, one hopes because they are so occasionally met with—were full of knick-knacks which threatened to fall over on the slightest provocation. Picture the two unhappy men in such surroundings—the preacher perched on the edge of a chair, afraid to move for fear of knocking something down: the farmer in agony in his morning coat of antique design. The preacher thought: 'This is his drawing-room, but in it he is like a fish out of water: he never uses it, hates the sight of it, has never made it his own, does not possess it and doesn't want to.'

The farmer thought: 'I wonder if this preacher is human. How can I get out of here?'

The preacher said: 'For the love of Mike let's go out into the kitchen—you'd be much more comfortable in your shirt-sleeves.'

The farmer said: 'Thank God!'

I was the preacher. That was one of my most successful week-ends.

Look, for contrast, at another room, this time the library of a scholar, friend of a friend of mine. Every wall is lined with books from floor to ceiling and the owner knows where every book is; and what is more, knows what is in every book. But the most remarkable thing is that the books stand two deep on the shelves—one behind the other —so that there is a hidden library behind the one you see. And he knows where all those are too, and what is in them.

No one could say that man did not possess his library.

In it he was in heaven; he used it, loved it, made it his own, gloried in it. Not of him could one say he was heir to much but possessor of little. He certainly knew how rich he was.

It does not, of course, matter very much whether the farmer possesses his drawing-room, not even (though this is more serious) whether the scholar possesses his library. But it is really tragic when, in the realm of the spirit, we limit ourselves by fastening upon a fragment when all things are ours. For the harm done is not confined to the merely negative result of our accomplishing less than we might have done: there is a subtle effect upon ourselves which makes us dishonest and self-acquitting when we might have been sincere and self-critical.

We have already looked at a curious little story Jesus once told of a business man who found it necessary to go abroad for a while and naturally did not want his business to evaporate while he was away. We have seen how he rewarded the men who showed drive and initiative, but we did not touch upon the third man.

He was rather a dark horse. Didn't show his hand much. Inclined to be lazy. He was tried out with one talent: even if he was too idle to do anything but put it in the bank it would make its own interest, so he would lose nothing anyhow.

As things turned out, however, this last man was not only lazy, he was dull-witted—stupid in fact. He may have thought he was not given much of a chance (which was quite true), but he was blind to the resources which were actually his. He had far more to work with than the one talent, but he lacked nous. After all, his master was a well-known merchant, and even if you have only a small job to do, if you are representing a well-known house, the very name of your firm can get you an opening if you know how to use it. And, anyway, there will be a list of customers to

start with, so that he would have *some* contacts ready made
surely. If it be objected that this is unjustifiably modernizing
the story by transplanting it into a twentieth-century commercial atmosphere, it may be replied that the point is in
no way lost or even weakened. He remains the typical
illustration of the man who limits himself by not using all
the resources at his command—and that is what Jesus was
driving at.

The judgement upon him is simply crushing. 'Take the
talent from him. Give it to him who has ten. For to every
one that hath (vision) shall be given (opportunity) and he
shall have abundance: but from him that hath not (initiative)
shall be taken away even that (unused trading capital) which
he seemeth to have.' There is all the difference in the world
—we see it again—between having and seeming to have;
between possessing and merely having available.

It behoves us, therefore, to make ourselves alive to the
resources of spiritual power at our disposal. One wonders
just what sort of powerful influence even the humblest of
us might wield if we did but realize how rich we are. And
since, in the previous chapter and in this we have been thinking a good deal about the enrichment of soul that comes to us
through the medium of our fellow men, I want to explore
just a little farther along that line. When you come to
think of it, you have received by far the greater part of
your knowledge of God from other men and women. They
have learnt in hard schools how God helps you out, and
when they tell you their story they speak from first-hand
experience and you learn something more of God than your
own experience has taught you so far. And, then, perhaps,
comes your own evil day and you remember how God stood
by your friend and you gain confidence that He will not let
you down either.

That is why it is the height of folly to close your mind to
some particular person's contribution to what might be

your spiritual treasure—on this stupid principle of 'I am of Paul, I of Apollos, I of Cephas, I of Christ'. Draw upon them all—all things are yours.

A great army have endowed you with a boundless heritage, just as all their great ministers had endowed the Church at Corinth. These men were not competitors, like candidates at an election, they were co-workers, each complementing the work of the others, and the combined contributions of them all were given to the Church as its working capital. They were given the solid ground-work teaching of Paul, the cultured eloquence of Apollos, and Peter's first-hand reminiscences of his Lord—all three of these privileges—to trade with and by their use of them to extend the business of the Kingdom of God. These were the talents put into their hands. But they too, like the merchant's lazy servant, were utterly blind to the fact that in addition to their working capital—their knowledge *about* Jesus—they had, for the very taking, the power of the Master they were to represent, the 'openings' which His previous transactions could give them, the impression His name had already made. But instead of *trading* with their faith they were content to argue about it—a futile business. Small wonder that Paul finds it hard to keep his patience with them, for what a contrast do they present to his own vivid example. How constantly was he trading with his knowledge of Jesus. Never did he lose an opportunity of telling of that wonderful experience upon the Damascus Road. He was a representative and he made the most of the reputation of his Master; made the most, too, of the previous transactions of His Lord: 'What He has done for me He can do for you.' Because he was Christ's, all the resources of Christ were at his command, just as a commercial traveller feels all the backing of his firm; and because Christ was God's, all the resources of God were at his command— infinite, illimitable, inexhaustible. Hear his exultant note:

'I can do all things' because in the realm of spiritual resources 'all things are mine'. This man is a born adventurer, a merchant-adventurer—and his merchandise is his Faith. This is not a thing to be buried in a napkin: it is to be traded with.

What, then, of us? For it is as true of us as of those Corinthian folk that 'all things are ours'. More so, indeed, for have we not another twenty centuries' knowledge of the ways of God? Have you ever tried to reckon up the spiritual capital which has been entrusted to you? Do you realize how rich you are?

Do you remember that man or that woman whose very fineness of disposition and character made you resolve to live better than ever before? How they stimulated your ideals and spurred on your enthusiasm for good things. How they came into your life with all this inspiring encouragement, opening to you their storehouse of spiritual treasure and saying 'all things are yours'.

Think of the great folk you have known who have lived through pain and ill health. Do you remember going to see them, full of sympathy yet wondering what on earth you would say when you got there? And you found in the sick-room a radiance which made you catch your breath and feel almost that you ought to take off your shoes, for you stood in a holy place. Has not your life been enriched by these Greathearts? Do they not teach you tremendous things about understanding the hard parts of life's journey? And do they not open to you the wealth of their own strange experience and all that they have learnt through it, and bid you learn, too, how to travel through the wilderness with your face ever towards the sun-rising? They also say to you 'all things are yours—all of God that I have come to know; the certainty of His everlasting arms underneath; His song in the night when the waves and billows are gone over me—all these things you may have: all are yours'.

Think of the folk who have cared for you, prayed for you, worked with you—believed in you when, perhaps, few did, and so steadied you at a difficult time. That was a lovely touch of a man who always paused a moment upon his own doorstep before entering his home, and said grace. He was thinking not of food but of fellowship—of his wife's smile and cheery greeting, of the bairns romping to meet him, even of the dog joining in the welcome as only a dog can, of the old familiar room and the many little evidences of preparation for his coming—thinking of these things he stayed a moment, hand on the door-knob, and said quietly: 'For what I am about to receive, Lord, accept my thanks.' Do they not speak to you of God, these homely joys?

And what of the friends who have stood by you in trouble? Humble folk, often enough, but they turn up as if by magic when anything goes wrong. How they get to know beats me. Or, if they live too far away, they take the trouble to write. Most of us have letters at home that we take out and read now and then until we put them away because the writing is becoming somewhat misty.

And what of those who have made demands upon you and thus given you the opportunity to let your soul come to the top? What of those who have challenged your thinking and so have driven you to crystallize your faith? Each in his own way has enriched your life. Each has contributed to your spiritual capital. All is yours.

Do you realize how rich you are? There is more yet.

Some of you who pick up this little book have an experience of your own of the power of Christ in your life. He has changed things for you. He has lifted burdens and come to you with His wondrous comfort on dark days. He has given you the thrill of fresh hope when your ambitions had turned to ashes. He has spoken to you things you could never tell anybody anything about. He has joined you on the road when faith was clean out and made your heart burn within you again. He has come up to where you sat with your head in your hands, beaten and defeated, and has set you on your feet again.

Now you are to trade with that: to adventure with it. You must not wrap that sort of thing up in a napkin. You must not bury an experience such as you have had. Nor must you limit your spiritual effectiveness by failing to claim what is yours for the asking. Moreover, you are to remember you are a representative. You are to trade with your faith with all the confidence which comes from realizing the resources at your back.

There is a queer little story told of the Navy at one of the bombardments of Sebastopol. At that time steam had just been brought into use for warships, and they had been fitted with auxiliary engines though still continuing to use their sails. In this particular engagement the British fleet was ordered to deploy, but one vessel took an unconscionably long time to manœuvre into position.

The Admiral signalled: 'Why don't you use your engines?' And provoked the reply: 'Forgot about the d—d things!'

There is no need to point the moral. But just to make sure, read again the title of this chapter.

CHAPTER XVII

ALL THE GOODNESS THERE IS

*'One is your Master, even Christ; and all ye are
brethren.'*

ONE of my favourite preachers when I was a young man
was the late Sydney B. Gregory. He was a shy, modest
man with nothing of the personally aggressive in his make
up. He had not the remotest idea of how to advertise his
own qualities—wasn't, indeed, at all interested—but at
proclaiming the qualities of his Lord I have heard few who,
in my judgement, were his equals. I remember him preaching
once about Christian Fellowship. It was during the First
World War when the question of unity of command of the
Allied Forces was a rather urgent issue. He developed the
idea that, whatever the Allies might decide, in the forces
of evil, at any rate, there is always unity of command. That,
of course, was not particularly new. But the implication he
drew from it was very refreshing indeed: namely, that when
any aggressive Christian work is afoot the Devil (we will
give him a capital D out of respect to his abilities and
enterprise) must re-distribute his forces to meet the situation. So it comes about that when you at your point in the
line are true to the best that you know, you break into the
ranks of evil and he must draw off some of his strength to
meet your attack. And this is the explanation of why it is
that when I, hard pressed at my point in the line, am just
on the point of yielding, there comes a sudden slackening
of the strain, a sudden easing of the pressure, which I
cannot understand, cannot account for, but which enables
me to hold out and win through.

Now this means, when you come to think it out, that you may receive spiritual help from people you do not even know and who do not know you, and conversely you may help someone quite unknown to you who may be having a very rough time hundreds of miles away. We have all known these occasions of unexpected relief when all seemed lost, but perhaps have never thought of some gallant soul flinging an extra effort into the battle, not with a view of helping you, for he doesn't know anything about you, but just to help the cause of the Kingdom of God. But the Devil cannot afford breaches in his line any more than we can, and must move his forces to meet the threatened points. This is where unity of command comes in—but the advantages are not all on his side.

So I would go back over the years to Sydney Gregory's sermon in order to conclude this list of the Christian's equipment, for one of the greatest of our assets is the simple faithfulness of other Christians: people we know and people we never heard of; people near and people far away; people of our own type and people of different classes, nationalities, colour, customs, and mental background. Wherever men and women strive for the things which are true, honourable, just, pure, lovely, and of good report, there is spiritual power in action and the powers of evil are engaged.

It seems a trite, almost an elementary thing to say that the goodness of all the Smiths, Browns, Jones's and Robinsons, and all the rest added together, comprises all the goodness there is in the world. 'Of course it is,' you say. 'Surely that is a foolish remark. How could there possibly be any more?' Exactly, how could there be? But there could be considerably less. It only needs you and me to live below our best for a while and the striking-power of goodness is weakened, that of evil is correspondingly increased, and the battle sways in favour of the enemy.

Nor is it any use to say that you can do so little that if you let up it will make no difference. You are not the best judge of that.

There is a strange story in the Old Book of a fierce battle fought out without quarter on a plain overlooked by a steep hill. On the hill-top, above the din and fury of the fight, are three men who watch intently the struggle as the fluctuating fortunes of the encounter sway the savage conflict to and fro. The centre figure of the little group is a venerable old man, but his every nerve is keyed up to follow the success or failure of his people. He sees them pressed back and raises his hands as invoking the help of God: they rally and fight grimly back, having, perhaps, caught a glimpse of his rugged figure summoning divine reinforcements to their aid, and as long as his hands are raised the battle sways their way. Tired, at length, the old man lowers his hands, and this the enemy notice and interpret to their own advantage: the gods are weary—an effort now and the day is won; and again the tide turns and the fight rolls back again over the trampled, blood-soaked plain. Again and again this happens —when the struggle continues beneath the raised hands of the old man Israel prevails; when his hands are weary and lowered, Amalek prevails. So it dawns upon the other two men on the hill-top that the issue of the battle is actually being decided by one who is not fighting. And once this great truth is grasped their course is clear. A great stone is rolled to the brow of the hill and the old man seated upon it; and on either side of him kneels a stalwart figure with the old man's forearm resting upon his shoulder, and his hands, thus supported, held out in blessing hour after hour.

'The gods are not weary—they fight against us!' cry the enemy, and begin to give ground.

'The Lord is among us!' cry the children of Israel—and the day is theirs.

Who really won the battle? The weary and wounded

warrior has no doubt; a rough and savage time he has had of it.

The stern old prophet on the hill, inspiring others to the limit of his strength likewise has no doubt. He feels himself the medium of morale and spiritual strength to his people—always an exhausting task to undertake.

Probably nobody ever gave a thought to the two men who held up the prophet's hands and kept them steady until the going down of the sun. Yet, one wonders, would the battle have been won without them? The striking-power of Israel was immediately concerned with their devotion to a very humble and unspectacular task. Amid the tumult in the valley there was no time to give a thought to the ways and means of strengthening the aged prophet on the hill-top. Yet if he failed all was lost. It is always the spirit of a nation that is the most important thing about it, always the men who sustain it who are the nation's greatest asset. But the spiritual leaders themselves have urgent need of support, and that is where you and I of the rank-and-file come in. So inextricably are we bound together that you cannot fail your Lord without handicapping your fellows. Nor, thank God, can we be faithful to the best we know without increasing the armed strength of those who fight a desperate warfare for truth on a part of the front we may never even know of.

Such, then, is the equipment with which you are furnished. You have a conception of the character of God which colours all life for you; you have a contented mind which, far from robbing you of all initiative, makes you ever a driving force and a pioneer spirit; you have a sense of power and of adequacy beyond all your wildest dreams; you have guidance in a score of different ways, giving you assurance and confidence; you have a wealth of resources in your fellow men and women, to say nothing of your own experience of God's dealings with you; and you have, finally, the whole of the active goodness in the world as your reinforcement.

Add to all this the plain horse-sense proposition that God would never set you to a task in which you were bound to fail, and surely you can face the future undismayed.

Well, as promised in our first chapter, you have looked at your problem and have stood aghast at it, no doubt; you have listened to your Lord and have been reassured; you have studied your equipment and have realized how you are fitted out. Now you are at the end of this little book and you lay it down. What you do next will determine whether you have found it worth reading.